Collecting Football Cards
for Fun and Profit

Collecting Football Cards
for Fun and Profit

How to buy, store, and trade them — and keep
track of their value as investments

Chuck Bennett with
Don Butler

Bonus Books, Inc., Chicago

95   94   93   92   91   5   4   3   2   1

Library of Congress Catalog Card Number: 91-72739

International Standard Book Number: 0-929387-32-5

Bonus Books, Inc.
160 East Illinois Street
Chicago, Illinois 60611

First Edition

Composition by Point West Inc., Carol Stream, IL

Printed in the United States of America

To my wife AnnClaire, thank you for the love and companionship you have provided me the past three years. And to my son, Alden, you have many years of card collecting ahead. I hope you will be as proud of your father as I am of mine.

C.B.

To Kim and Lauren, thank you for your love and support.

D.B.

Contents

Getting Started—A Look at Recent Football Card History

Five years ago, football cards were considered the weak sister of the sports card industry. There wasn't much diversity in selection—only one company, Topps, was making cards and issuing them on a national basis. A few teams were issuing their own regional team sets, but these cards didn't receive much attention. At card shows, few dealers actually carried old football cards at their tables. Information and interest in older football card sets was scarce.

Diehard football card collectors were not happy. First, Topps cut back the number of cards in its annual set from 528 to 396 in the early 1980s. Second, while rookie mania was taking hold in baseball (three companies—Topps, Donruss, and Fleer—were battling to see who could include the most rookies in its regular issue and update set), football cards still were a dead issue. Dan Marino, John Elway, and Eric Dickerson entered their third years in the league before Topps issued their rookie cards in 1984 (and as late as 1988, none of the three rookie cards were valued at more than

$2). A conservative estimate puts the sales of Topps football cards in 1986 at less than $20 million.

In 1989, as the story goes, things changed. Topps' football contract with NFL Properties was changed to admit new companies. This was stunning news to several young companies trying to break into the booming sportscard market. Football, arguably the most popular sport in America, could be somebody's key to the treasure chest.

Two more football licenses were granted in 1989. Pro Set, a tiny Dallas based outfit led by dynamic Lud Denny, issued a set backed by NFL Properties. Its Series I cards issued in May 1989 blew collectors away. Pro Set's affiliation with the NFL allowed it to tap into NFL Properties' awesome photo file. On any given Sunday, the NFL has as many as eighty photographers shooting a single NFL game. Pro Set's access to the file gave it some of the best game-action photos in the sportscard market. Topps had been using its own photographers for years, but the pictures used on the cards were generally posed shots, warm-up photos, or pictures of the players on the sidelines. The quality of photos on the Pro Set cards alone grabbed younger collectors and people who had never picked up cards before.

Pro Set incorporated another relatively new idea in its Series I issue—the four-color back. Score had begun the idea of using a full-color head shot of the player on its card backs a few years before and had won a loyal following of collectors who enjoyed action fronts and profile backs. Pro Set decided to try the same thing in football cards. That meant a thicker, glossier card stock than the simple two-color cardboard backing Topps had used for decades. Not only did the card backs improve, but the quality of card stock went up as well.

Three new developments: action fronts, full-color backs, and photos on the backs—and football card collecting had changed. The results revolutionized not only the football card market, but the entire hobby. The cards were gorgeous and collectors went crazy trying to find the cards.

However, Pro Set didn't just rest on its new reputation and wait for collectors to discover its cards. First, Pro Set produced millions of cards, many times the print run of any previous cards, to make sure everyone could find its cards practically everywhere. Second, Denny took his cards to collectors. Full-color ads spouting the wonders of Pro Set football cards appeared in the hobby publications. Pro Set took its people, cards, and a spiffy booth to the big card shows. The company mailed out *Pro Set Gazette*, a 16-page color magazine on Pro Set cards, free to anyone who wrote for one.

Another reason for Pro Set's initial success—and for some of the criticism leveled at the company—was its penchant for creating variations. If an error was found on a card or if a card needed updating, Pro Set stopped the printing press, corrected the card, and released the corrected version. This "living set" philosophy drove football card purists up a wall, but younger collectors didn't seem to mind searching for a potentially valuable card as they cleaned out retailer's shelves across the country.

Pro Set football cards had been issued four months earlier than Topps' usual release date, and the cards looked better than ever and were produced in larger quantities than ever before. Suddenly, football cards were everywhere, as Pro Set targeted not only baseball card collectors, but potential first-time collectors.

In July, the second new football card company made its debut.

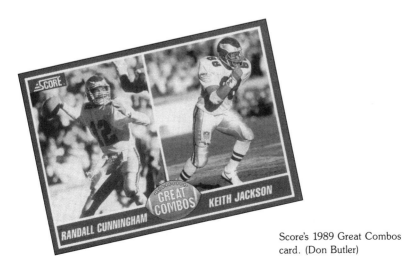

Score's 1989 Great Combos card. (Don Butler)

For its 1989 set, Score tracked down Deion Sanders (then with the N.Y. Yankees) in his Milwaukee hotel for this card. (Don Butler)

Score, which had impressed collectors with the quality of its two base-ball sets, brought the same knockdown approach to football. Like Pro Set, full-color photos appeared on the fronts and backs of the cards. Score introduced two more concepts to football cards: exciting sub-sets and same-year rookie cards. Subsets were not a new idea, as Topps had used numerous subsets over the years. Score merely up-graded the quality of the subsets in its football set, introducing "Great Combos" (Randall Cunningham/Keith Jackson, Joe Montana/Jerry Rice), and new photos and different cards for All-Pro players.

But by far the new addition that caught collector attention was the inclusion of cards for the 1989 first-round draft picks. Score worked most of the spring and summer to set up photos with each of that year's first-rounders, getting each to pose in a baseball cap of the team that drafted him. Deion Sanders, for instance, was on a road trip with the New York Yankees, with whom he was playing, in early summer. Score tracked him down in a hotel room in Milwaukee and had him pose with an Atlanta Falcons baseball cap. The process of obtaining photos was complicated by the fact that many of the players were unsigned and Score had to work with the rookies through their agents to set up the shots. But it was more than worth it, as Score cards were completely sold out in a few months.

In two short months, football cards grew up. As in baseball, the photos were exciting and the rookies had appeared. What else could happen?

Plenty, as it turned out. Pro Set further intrigued the market in October 1989 by issuing a Series II of 100 cards (about four Series II cards appeared with 11 Series I cards in "updated" wax packs), which—like Score—also featured first-round 1989 draft picks. Pro Set's Series II went a step further and included "Pro Set Prospects," lower-round picks from the 1989 draft. Pro Set also included football's first same-year "traded" cards of players who switched teams during the 1989 training camps and pre-season.

Score came back a month later with football's first true "update set," a boxed set sold only in hobby stores which, like Pro Set's Series II, included overlooked players and traded players. One of the cards in the set was a promotional photo Bo Jackson did for Nike shoes. It shows him bare-chested, wearing football shoulder pads, and carrying a baseball bat over his shoulder. The black-and-white photo quickly became 1989's first $20 card.

Topps, taken by surprise, went almost unnoticed when its cards came out in August. The company tried to capitalize on the football card explosion with its own 132-card update set in January. Topps also included most of the 1989 first-round picks, such as Barry Sanders, Tony Mandarich, and supplemental pick Bobby Humphrey. Like Score's update set, the cards were available only in hobby shops. The cards sold well, but probably not as well as they should have. A lot of younger collectors were turned off by the "typical Topps photos" which, in the case of Barry Sanders, showed the 1989 Rookie of the Year sitting on the bench.

Pro Set had the last word in the 1989 football card deluge, as it issued a "Final Update" of twenty cards randomly distributed in Series II wax packs and through a mail-in offer. These twenty players included more traded players, and guys not included in the first two series—either overlooked or unsigned by Pro Set.

Many people in the hobby point to 1989 as the turning point for football cards, and for all non-baseball cards in general. The impact

This 1976 Walter Payton
rookie card rose from $40
to $100 within two months
in 1989. (Don Butler)

the two new companies had on the hobby can't be denied, but collectors caught wind of big things in the football card market even before
Pro Set's first Series I box was shipped.

In late 1988 and early 1989, the prices on older football cards
began to rise as collectors began seeking them out. The prices weren't
tremendous when we look back now, but at the time a steady rise in
the value of football cards was unheard of. A Jimmy Brown rookie
card, which for years had been valued at less than $50, rose to
around $90 by June 1989. The price tag on Walter Payton's rookie
card changed from $40 to $75 to $100 in three months. The 1952
Bowman Large football set, considered to be "high-end" at $750 for
the complete set, tripled in price in a few weeks. And the Joe Namath rookie card, which could be found in 1988 for less than $100,
was approaching the $200 mark by the time Pro Set made its debut.
Booming sales were helping to stir interest in older football cards. In
the summer and fall of 1989, dealers could not keep enough older
football cards in stock.

Why did prices rise on older football cards even before the new

1965 Topps Joe Namath rookie card. You could've bought it for less than $100 in 1988. (Don Butler)

1989s were issued? The most logical explanation has to do with baseball cards. For years the interest in baseball cards had resulted in steadily rising prices of older cards. Collectors trying to piece together older sets simply could not afford to do so after awhile as card values essentially priced them out of the hobby. Many looked to other more affordable sports collectibles to buy and found football the perfect antidote—almost as much history and popularity as baseball cards, but generally a fifth of the price. Football cards also made an obvious investment vehicle, since they were made in far less quantity than baseball cards.

We'd guess that for a given year before 1985, the amount of football cards produced was anywhere from 80 to 90 percent lower than the amount of baseball cards. If Topps produced 50 million baseball cards one year, for example, the company might produce 5 to 10 million football cards. Scarcity, as we'll discuss elsewhere in this book, makes collectors take notice.

Fleer returned to football player cards for the first time in more than twenty years. (Don Butler)

The 1990 football collecting season saw a couple new entrants in the game—Fleer and Action Packed. The collectors wondered what else could possibly happen, as five companies struggled for a piece of the football market.

For years, Fleer had released a set of 88-card "action" sets which could only show pro offenses and defenses but could not identify players. Its first full-fledged football issue in 1990 became the hottest cards of the year—and distribution problems, with some pockets of the country getting lots of the cards and some areas getting none, only fueled the fire.

Fleer had basically ignored the sportscard hobby for years, but when it was taken over by a publicly held firm in 1989, new people with new attitudes arrived. Fleer CEO Paul Mullan, who was refreshingly candid, told *Sports Collectors Digest,* "We expect to come out as the number two manufacturer (in terms of production) in the hobby. We expect to be behind Pro Set and our objective is to be above Topps and Score in terms of number of cards produced. I am not in this business, as much as I appreciate the hobby side of the business, to pass products by the kids."

Action Packed introduced a couple of developments which further defined the football card market. The first was the production of a truly high-end card aimed at the well-to-do collector. Cards were embossed and lacquered, meaning the player actually stood out from the rest of the card. The backs featured an "Action Note"—information on the play from which the photo on the front of the card was taken. The backs of the Action Packed cards included an autograph line, thus encouraging collectors to get signatures of their favorite players. From the outset, Action Packed knew it had to reach a different audience. The production costs alone meant higher prices on cards. Packs generally went for $2.50 and contained six cards, which did not attract the casual collector. To make sure it sold, Action Packed produced only some 35,000 sets, hoping that the set's scarcity and high quality would bring about good sales.

Meanwhile, Score and Pro Set continued with successful formulas in 1990. Lots of rookies, lots of great photos. The outstanding sales continued into 1990 as well, as each company really began to crank out the cards. Pro Set, which started with three employees, had more than 1,500 only fifteen months after its first boxes of cards were released; Lud Denny's company made an estimated $100 million in 1990.

The major companies were not the only ones in the spotlight. More and more teams became involved in regional sets, such as police/safety cards handed out by local law enforcement officials. Football cards again began turning up in cereal boxes. Even the British market became a newfound target, as a United Kingdom television station released a 20-card set of all-time great NFL quarterbacks and Topps issued two small sets explaining American football to the British audiences.

Going into the 1990s, the picture for football collectors seems reasonably healthy. Despite a recession, sales appear to be doing better than they were in 1987 for football cards. Most of the card companies are financially healthy and are sure to be around for awhile, battling for their share of the collector's dollar. In 1991, more new companies joined the lineup, including Pacific, Upper Deck, Classic, and Star Pics. Some fourteen major card sets were produced.

Football cards are here to stay. Whether there are any more niches in the hobby that cards can explore will be discovered in the next few seasons.

It's an exciting time to collect football cards. In this book we'll give you some tips on what to look for and what to expect out of the hobby.

The History of Football Cards

While baseball cards are the oldest of the sports cards, appearing in tobacco issues in the mid-1880s, football also appeared before the turn of the century in the form of the 1890 Mayo Cut Plug cards.

The first cards as we know them were premium giveaways with tobacco. Thirty-six cards appeared in the set which featured collegiate players from Eastern schools such as Yale, Princeton, and Harvard. Including players from these Eastern schools makes sense because football was first played between Princeton and Rutgers University in New Jersey in the late 1880s.

The cards are crude by today's standards but they are quite significant because they were the first cards to promote the relatively new sport of football. There are no major stars who would open your eyes; the set is listed alphabetically with card number 36, an unidentified player, being the most valuable because it's the last card in the set. The photos were stills of the players in their collegiate uniforms. In fact they look like most of the other tobacco issues of the times but the players are wearing hooded

1990 Action Packed
Thurman Thomas. (Chuck
Bennett)

sweatshirts with big letters instead of uniforms. The cards measure $1^5/8'' \times 2^7/8''$ and have blank, black backs. It is safe to say that the set is rare (a tough word to use in this hobby), and by far one of the most important historical football issues printed.

It was almost another thirty years before the second football set would appear. The Sports Company of America produced a 102-card set in 1926. The set was multi-sport and again the football players featured were collegiate stars. The California based company included mostly stars from the West Coast. A total of thirty-nine football cards were produced in this first ever non-tobacco issue that measured $1^1/2'' \times 3''$.

Athletes from several sports were featured in the 1933 Goudey Sport Kings issue. Besides greats from other sports, the legendary Red Grange, Knute Rockne, and Jim Thorpe appear in gridiron uniforms. These $2^3/8'' \times 2^7/8''$ cards were strictly a bubble gum issue and are a very popular set today.

Two years later the first bubble gum issued set dedicated entirely to football appeared under the heading of National Chicle. Highlight-

1957 Topps Richard Lane.
(Chuck Bennett)

ing this 36-card set are former football greats Rockne and the first ever card of Bronko Nagurski. The cards measure $2^3/8'' \times 2^7/8''$ and are beautiful full-color cards much like the early Diamond Star baseball cards.

Prior to the discovery of the Mayo and Sports Company set, the National Chicle set was thought to be the first major football card release. It also gets more publicity than either of the first two mentioned because of the big names and Hall of Famers among its thirty-six cards.

Another gap in football card production appeared and collectors had to wait until 1948 for the next football issue. But what a year. In 1948, both the Leaf Gum Company and the Bowman Company produced football card sets. Bowman produced the larger of the two sets, 108 cards in all.

The 1948 Bowman black and white beauties are among the hottest collectibles today. Because of the number of cards and the types of printing sheets used, the 1948 set has a number of short printed

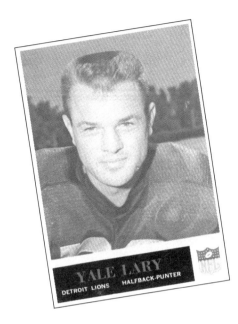

1965 Philadelphia's Yale
Lary. (Chuck Bennett)

cards—the divisible by three cards to be exact. The divisible by three
cards (3/6/9/12/15. . .) have a price tag of five to six times greater
than the other cards because of their scarcity. Nearly every card in the
set is considered a rookie card with some of the greatest names in the
modern post-war era included. Guys like Johnny Lujack, Charley
Conerly, Sammy Baugh, and Sid Luckman thrilled crowds as professional football began to catch on across the nation.

Leaf was a bit more ahead of its time and issued a hand-colored
set of ninety-eight players. Many of the same players who were included in the Bowman set made the Leaf set as well. The Leaf cards
from 1948 are generally harder to find than the Bowman cards of
that same year.

Bowman dropped out of the card race in 1949; no definite reason why is known, but it was up against the stiff competition of the
four-color Leaf cards. Also in 1949, Leaf released a set with an interesting twist. The cards in the 1949 Leaf set were numbered through
150, but there were just forty-nine cards in the set. According to
some information gathered, Leaf thought it would sell more cards if it

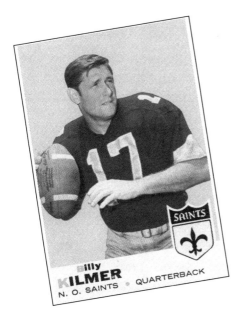

1969 Topps Billy Kilmer.
(Chuck Bennett)

skipped a few numbers. Leaf did this in hope that collectors would think they were missing a few numbers and continue buying Leaf cards.

Before the 1949 season was over collectors were asking a lot of questions and when word came out that Leaf had deliberately skipped numbers in the set, collectors were turned off by the ploy. Even today many novice collectors are relieved to find out that their set that they once thought was incomplete is really whole. Again, the 1949 set is loaded with Hall of Famers and stars like Luckman, Charley Trippi, Bobby Layne, and Chuck Bednarik.

The start of a new decade (1950) also meant the return of the Bowman football cards. In 1950 the company released a 144-card set that closely resembles the 1949 Bowman baseball cards. The hand-colored cards are among the most fabulous cards ever produced. The printing quality and the color reproduction were way ahead of their time. Bowman clearly established itself on top of the card world. Again Hall of Famers and stars trickle through this set like Barry Sanders through an opposing defense. Rookies in the 1950 set include: Doak Walker, Y. A. Tittle, Lou Groza, Glenn Davis, Marion Motley, Otto Graham, and Elroy Hirsch.

Topps entered the game, trying something new in 1950. Remembering that collegiate football was still king of the hill during this period, Topps released a 100-card set referred to as the "feltback set."

The cards were unusual in size ($^7/_8'' \times 1^7/_{16}''$) and were divided into four color groups: red, blue, green, and purple. Each color group had twenty-five cards, but a yellow felt back group of twenty-five was also made, (possibly at the same time), making for some interesting variations.

The fronts of the cards display the player's photo along with name and team identification while the backs of the cards have felt depicting a college pennant. The most popular card in the set would be the Joe Paterno card if not for the great interest in the Jackie but Jenson yellow felt card. Not a star who has enjoyed the success that Paterno has on the gridiron, but Jenson is the best known of the yellow variation cards. Other notables in the set include: Leon Hart, Charlie Justice, Leo Nomellini, Darrell Royal, Doak Walker, and Ernie Stautner.

1968 Topps Matt Snell.
(Chuck Bennett)

In 1951 Bowman changed its design. The design changes included a team logo, and the player's name on the front of the card. Bowman did keep the 144-card set. The beautiful hand-colored reproduction was also still evident. Key cards in the set include Norm Van Brocklin, Tom Landry, Emlen Tunnell, and Ernie Stautner.

Topps continued to work with collegiate players and in 1951 released another oddball set. This time Topps dropped the felt back and opted for the standard information backs which included a scratch-off quiz. Thus because of the oddity, the 1951 Topps set is known as the "Magic Set."

Seventy-five of the country's best collegiate players grace these $2^{1}/_{16}'' \times 2^{15}/_{16}''$ cards. Babe Parilli, Marion Campbell, and Heisman winner Vic Janowicz are the best known players in the set. Because both the 1950 and 1951 Topps set aren't mainstream, many collectors find them uncollectible and thus they are not on the top of the want list, although they still demand a high price when they are purchased.

Bowman must have cornered the market in these early days because Topps dropped out of the football card market after the 1951 season and did not return until 1955.

Bowman produced some of its most beautiful work in these early years. In 1952 Bowman produced two sets of the same cards. Again these were artistic in nature and generally are recognized as the Bowman Large and the Bowman Small set. The Bowman Small set was the first to be released. The dimensions of the cards were $2^{1}/_{16}'' \times 3^{1}/_{8}''$.

For some reason later in the year, Bowman released the same picture cards on a $2^{1}/_{2}'' \times 3^{3}/_{4}''$ stock. Some believe that Bowman was getting ready for its upcoming baseball card season and it was experimenting with a new size. Either way Bowman did enlarge the size of its 1952 baseball set from the previous 1951 year.

The 1952 Large set is one of the toughest sets to complete and the price of the set has risen dramatically during the recent football card craze.

Bowman went on to produce sets in 1953, 1954, and 1955 before the company was purchased by Topps, which at the time ceased to make any other cards under the Bowman name. Topps issued baseball cards under the Bowman name in 1989.

Topps hit the scene again in 1955 and it continued to work with

1955 Bowman Dorne
Dibble. (Chuck Bennett)

the collegiate stars, but this time it took no chance, as stars of great magnitude were included in the set. Guys like Knute Rockne, the Four Horseman, Jim Thorpe, and Sammy Baugh made up the set. Today it is known as the Topps All-American set.

In 1956, Topps switched and decided to go with professional players and the rest, as they say, is history; Topps has produced football card sets for the NFL every year since.

Topps did have a competitor every now and then. In 1960, Fleer broke on the scene with an AFL set of 132 cards, including the Jack Kemp rookie card. Fleer also produced sets in 1961, 1962, and 1963. Consistency was not the Fleer game plan. In 1961, Fleer's set jumped to 220 cards but fell to 88 in 1962 and finished with 89 in 1963.

With Fleer out of the picture, the Philadelphia Gum Company would try their luck at unseating Topps. The Philadelphia sets ran from 1964 through 1967. Unlike Fleer, Philadelphia went with the more established NFL and still could not survive.

During the period between 1964 through 1967, Topps decided

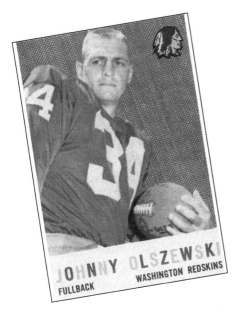

1959 Topps Johnny
Olszewski. (Chuck Bennett)

to go with the AFL cards instead of the more established NFL card. A tough corporate decision, but Topps struck it big in 1965 with the printing of the Joe Namath rookie card. Card number 122 in the 1965 set is to football collectors what the 1952 Mickey Mantle is to baseball collectors. Topps picked up the NFL license in 1967 and has continued to issue NFL cards ever since.

Topps finished the 1960s in style and ran through the 1970s with no major competition. There are many highly sought after cards from the 1970s, none more so than the 1972 high number set. Cards numbered 1 through 263 in this set are relatively easy to get but trying to get cards 264 through 351 is a nightmare. Topps printed this third series of cards in very low numbers and then, when it got to be late in the 1972 season, they "dumped" them to one dealer who has been the major supplier of 1972 high numbers since.

One of the best single cards of the 1970s was the 1976 rookie Walter Payton card which saw a serious increase in value when Payton became the NFL's all-time leading rusher.

The early 1980s weren't so good for football card collectors or

1955 Topps All-American
Ed Franco. (Chuck
Bennett)

Topps. In 1981, both Donruss and Fleer hit the baseball scene. While that was great for baseball card collectors, less attention was directed towards the sport we love and Topps seemed to be focusing less on detail and design than in the past. In 1983, the football set was a 1980s low of 396 cards, and while there were some great players to appear in this decade—something was lacking.

Nineteen eighty-nine was one of the most significant years in football card history. A close look will show you exactly why it was such an important year.

Not only did Pro Set and Score hit the football card collectors like a lead weight but they also challenged the authority and dominance of Topps. Football collectors came out of their shells in 1989 to gobble up the new cards. People who collected cards of just their favorite player or team became full-time legitimate football card collecting fanatics.

The quality of football cards rose to a new level. Update sets were introduced to the football collectors for the first time and, in general, the hobby business was turned upside down in a very short period.

In 1990, both Fleer and Action Packed joined the growing football card market. Today collectors have their choice of Action Packed, Classic, Fleer, Fleer Ultra, Pacific, Pro Set, Score, Star Pics, Stars in Stripes, Topps, Stadium Club, and Upper Deck.

Who and What to Collect

The most common question among new football card collectors is, "What should I collect?"

That's easy. Collect ANYTHING YOU WANT.

"But I also want to make money on the side," they say.

Not to chastise, but if you go into the hobby with an investor-only attitude, you're almost bound to lose money.

First, you have to accept that football cards, like baseball and other sports cards, are only pieces of cardboard with photos on them. They carry no intrinsic value. The value is derived from the demand of the card by other collectors. And collector whim, though usually dependent upon the performance of a player, is not immune to outside factors.

Brian Bosworth, for example, had a rookie card in the 1987 Topps set once valued at $4. Despite the rapid advances in most other football prices, his card held steady and then fell, eventually hitting bottom at the 50-cent mark when it was learned in 1990 that his career was over. (Despite all that, Bosworth's card prices may take a phoenix-like rise if his Hollywood career blossoms as the "Loud One" hopes.)

Deion Sanders, though he has shown just a few flashes of greatness, has one of the higher-priced rookie cards in the 1989 Score football set. The demand exists mainly because of his 1989 two-sport popularity and his incredible efforts at publicizing himself. If Sander's baseball career falters or if he continues to show little progress on the gridiron, his card values will almost surely drop.

Even before his career-threatening hip injury, Bo Jackson, who has quite a bit more talent than Sanders, was not considered by us to be a very good investment. After his injury, his 1988 Topps rookie card fell from $20 to $8.

Another example is Packer offensive lineman Tony Mandarich. Just before the 1989 NFL draft, *Sports Illustrated* ran a cover story on him, calling him the greatest offensive line prospect ever. Such hype drove the cost of his 1989 rookie card up to at least $1. After a long contract holdout, he was unable to win a starting job in 1989 with Green Bay, and he showed little progress in 1990. His cards have since dropped in value. Fame is pretty fleeting, especially when there's always another batch of rookies to watch for.

Football card collecting, in its basic form, is hero worship. People buy the cards to see their favorite player in action and to read about his accomplishments on the card back. But fans are always fickle, and heroes rise and fall quickly in sports today.

Joe Charboneau. Darryl Dawkins. David Thompson. Ricky Jordan. Ickey Woods. Jerome Walton. All these players had cards that were hot for a short period of time, before injury or a return to mortal form doomed them in sports collectors' eyes.

Back to the original premise. Collect whatever you want to collect—teams, a specific player, food issued sets, complete sets. Here's a rundown of what to look for and what to expect in each collecting category.

1. COMPLETE SETS.

This means collecting each card printed by a specific company in a particular year. Cards can be collected through the purchase of wax boxes, where you open the packs yourself and try to

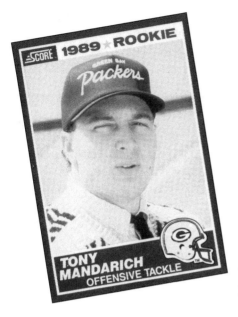

Tony Mandarich's 1989
Score card, once at $1.50,
has fallen to fifty cents.
(Don Butler)

complete a set on your own, by buying a complete set from a dealer, or by buying a factory set from the company.

A factory set is simply a complete set that the factory puts together and makes available to you through a retail store, such as ShopKo or Wal-Mart, or through hobby dealers. These sets cost about the same as a hand-collated set, but usually come in a fancy box created by the card company. In 1990, only three companies—Topps, Score, and Action Packed—produced factory sets, so about half the companies still encourage you to make a set from packs.

It's a good idea to plan when you buy your factory set, because card companies often release more than one factory set per year. For example, in 1989, Score released two different factory sets of its football cards. In the later editions, Score corrected nine cards, and these have become fairly valuable since most collectors bought the early print run of the factory set. (Obviously, you can't predict if a company will go back to press to correct its mistakes and include them in factory sets, but if you find out about late-run corrections available in factory sets, it's *always* a good idea to get a late-run version, even if you have the first-run factory set.) Another reason for planning your factory set purchase is the ever changing value. When factory sets are first released, demand is pretty high and a set can cost quite a bit of money. After a month or two, when other cards capture collector interest, the price will usually come down a few bucks. A few months after that is a key time for the value of a factory set (or for any set, for that matter). If a lot were made and buyers are lukewarm toward it, the price will drop even further. If collectors believe it's scarce and spend a lot of time looking for it, the value will shoot back up. It's wise to keep an eye on what's happening in the hobby.

Compiling a set yourself, obviously, is what the card hobby is based upon. When you buy packs of cards or boxes of cards, the thrill is in opening the packs, finding a favorite player, and perhaps finding valuable doubles for trading or selling.

If you're on a budget, though, buying a complete set from a dealer cuts out a lot of the extra expense. For example, you might need three boxes of 1990 Topps cards to complete the football set. The cost of a wax box might be around $15, so you could spend $45 to complete a set of Topps. If you don't have $45 but want the set, you could find one through a dealer for $20 or so and save your money for some other cards.

On the plus side, you save yourself $25. On the minus side, suppose you did buy three boxes of 1990 Topps and after sorting through all 1,628 cards, you came up with six Andre Ware rookie cards. Then suppose that two years down the road, Andre Ware takes Detroit to the Super Bowl and starts in the Pro Bowl two weeks later. Also suppose Topps cards somehow become the vogue item for collectors to buy. Collectors discover 1990 Topps had one of the shortest print runs of the 1990 issues, and the Andre Ware 1990 Topps rookie card is one of the highest priced 1990 issues at $25 a card. Now, if you'd bought only factory sets, the price on it would have risen accordingly, to maybe $40 to $45 or so, reflecting the increase in Ware's value and in the value of the 1990 set, so you made twenty to twenty-five bucks. But if you bought wax boxes, your original $45 investment has already seen a profit of $105, not counting the other stars you doubtlessly pulled out of the 1990 Topps wax.

That's the dilemma. Do you buy factory sets and assure yourself of having a set? If you're a strict collector, don't have the extra money for wax boxes, and you want to have a complete collection; the answer is yes. If you're partial to investing, can afford to buy wax boxes, and firmly believe a particular issue will rise in value; then you're better off buying the wax boxes. The decision, obviously, is a tough one, since nobody knows how card values will perform.

2. TEAM SETS.

Nowhere near as popular as collecting complete sets, the team collecting category is one of the oldest and purest forms of the hobby. Team set collectors acquire a stockpile of cards from a particular year to trade with other collectors in return for a player on his favorite team.

Team set collectors rarely view their acquisitions from just a monetary angle. They collect memorabilia because they root for a specific team. As a rule, you rarely see a large team collection enter the hobby unless a guy's completely broke or it's an estate sale.

Say a guy is a Cleveland Browns collector. He might be willing to trade a Joe Montana card for a same-year Bernie Kosar issue. The values are quite different, but to a team collector who really wants the Kosar card, Montana doesn't mean much to him and is a fair trade.

That doesn't mean you should take team collectors as idiots. Team collectors know full well the values of football cards; to them, acquiring complete sets of their favorite teams is the object. Team collectors usually acquire other memorabilia, such as programs, autographs and photos, to round out their collections.

Team set collectors try to get every issue affiliated with their team. A Seattle Seahawk team collector will undoubtedly try to acquire a police/safety set of his team, though the current value of police sets isn't that great compared to regular nationally issued football cards.

3. SPECIFIC PLAYERS.

These collectors, who are usually team set collectors as well, are after any card or piece of memorabilia of a certain player. If he's a Walter Payton fan, he'll already have every regular issue card of the NFL's all-time leading rusher; he may be looking for such items as the Chicagoland Processing Corporation's limited edition Walter Payton set or a 1978 Topps Holsum Bread card of Payton. If he's acquired those, he might be after out-of-print posters or old sports magazines featuring Payton on the cover.

4. ROOKIE CARDS.

For about the past five years, the biggest craze in the hobby has been rookie cards. Between 1987 and 1990, according to several sources, no other commodity provided as great an initial return on the original investment as star rookie cards—both old and new rookie cards.

Johnny Unitas' rookie card, in decent shape, went from maybe $75 to at least $900 in about a year. Jim Brown's rookie card, stuck at just under $50 for more than three years, can bring a value of about $600 in Near Mint condition. You could've talked a dealer out of a Joe Namath rookie card for under $80 not three years ago; but if you can find one in Near Mint shape for under $1,200, you've found a decent deal. In the summer of 1989, Score wax and factory sets were everywhere and you could've purchased Barry Sanders rookies all day at $1 to $2. Today, the set is the scarcest of the popular 1989 releases, and nobody's selling rookie cards of Mr. Sanders for under $35.

More than any other segment of the hobby, the rookie card phenomenon is investor- and speculator-driven. In most of the hobby press, you can find dozens of ads for dealers selling 100-count lots of this year's hot rookies. Rookie card collectors/investors buy the cards and, in most cases, keep them in their closet without even opening the package to see what they look like. They'll be sold for a substantial profit when they feel the time is right.

1989 Pro Set's Barry Sanders rookie — huge production numbers kept value down until 1991. (Don Butler)

Is it safe to buy/invest in rookie cards? These days it's just not as rewarding as it was three years ago. Today's companies are keenly aware of the increased demand in cards and consequently produce more cards. More cards means people can buy more, so there's less demand. The value attached to a particular rookie in 1992 should conceivably not be as great as the value for a similar rookie in 1988.

Decreased value on rookie cards is quite apparent in the 1990 issues. Pro Set had by far the largest production numbers of any card manufacturer. If you compare prices of such rookies as Andre Ware, Blair Thomas, and Jeff George to a company with a smaller print run, such as Score or Fleer, you'll find a difference of a quarter or more.

The same thing is true of the 1989 sets. Pro Set put out an incredible amount of cards—possibly more than Topps and Score combined. Because of that, the Pro Set Barry Sanders card held its $7.50 price tag while the same-year Score Sanders rookie climbed from $12 to $30.

We're willing to say that after 1989 Score, no subsequent major football set may demand such high prices for rookie cards so soon after its release. Why? Again, companies know they can sell a lot of cards and make more money, so they make a lot of cards. Print runs will never be that low again. Be careful if you decide to sink serious money into same-year rookie cards.

But in 1991, there companies produced cards with low print runs: Pacific, Star Pics, and Classic. All three sets bear watching.

5. HIGH-END CARDS.

"High-end" usually means older cards in Near Mint or better condition. The name alone should tip you off to the fact it takes a lot of money to go after these cards.

This category is also the realm of the investor. There are thousands of new people each year who enter the hobby and spend several hundred dollars on rookie cards of a particular player—a Troy Aikman, a Jeff George, a Blair Thomas—in the hopes the player does well and the card eventually makes a few hundred (or a few thousand) dollars over the course of three to five years. Between 1989 and 1990, football investors who wanted a quick turn around on their money and ended up with $100-plus profit returns per card turned to high-end cards.

When we say "older" or "high-end" cards, we're primarily referring to cards before, say, 1970. Football cards are estimated to be up to eight times scarcer than baseball cards during the pre-1970 years. Baseball cards have always been the "glamor" collectible and have always sold well; football cards have always been a very poor second, sold only to those hardy souls who feverishly collected cards on a seasonal basis.

Especially difficult to find "major" cards for are the National Chicles from 1935 and the Leaf/Bowman/Topps/Fleer issues from the late 1940s through the early 1960s. Those who actually collected cards from those years rarely stored them well or even kept them at all, which explains the scarcity and lousy condition of

1935 National Chicle's Bronko Nagurski — at more than $4,500 this is one of the football card hobby's most valuable cards. (Don Butler)

those you find today. More often than not, the cards ended up between the spokes of a bike or at the bottom of a garbage can. Cards that were saved were rubber-banded together, tossed in desk drawers, or suffered such hideous fates as being glued into scrapbooks, pinned to walls, used as scratch pads, or folded up like Kleenex in back pockets.

Only when collectors banded together in the mid-1970s and realized it was a good idea to avoid destroying cards, were proper storage techniques followed. (More on this in chapter 11.) By then, it was too late for the older stuff; relatively few survived.

When the 1989 football card boom hit, old football cards began appearing side-by-side in dealers' display cases. Those smart enough to follow the trend picked up as many cards in Near Mint or better condition—high-end cards—as they could. Bart Starr and George Blanda rookie cards in near mint condition might have been as high as $100 in 1989. Those who could afford the price bought lots of cards and had to wait only a year or less to quadruple their original investment.

For high-end investors and collectors, the best thing about this segment of the hobby is its relative immunity from the factors that affect post-1970s cards. A 1990 rookie has a great season, his cards go up in price; someone thinks they'll make a killing and buys 100 at $5 each. Two weeks later, the player blows out a knee or is benched and the price drops to fifty cents a card. Goodbye, $450.

That type of uncertainty and fluctuation will never occur for high-end cards. For starters, there's almost no chance a player's pre-1970 card will drop in value once it has been set. The player is retired; his gridiron deeds have been duly listed. The only direction a high-end card will go in value is up. If the player makes the Hall of Fame on an old-timer's ballot, his cards will rise in value. If he doesn't, they'll at least remain at the established level.

As more and more collectors enter the hobby, many are serious enough to continue working backward in their collection. As they look for older material, demand increases. The scarcity of older cards assures their values will be safe from a recession. Nothing short of a total collapse in the game of football or the card-collection market will bring the prices down.

Why would high-end cards hold value during a recession? Say a group of collectors has a lot of 1962 Topps cards in superb condition. They're getting antsy because the economic forecasters are predicting doom and gloom. They decide to sell all their cards now and sink their profits into Venetian blinds. They put the cards up for open auction. Bids start coming in; it's apparent the collectors have gotten out too late, as offers are for maybe half of what they expected.

Did they get out too late? A buyer with deep pockets has been watching and waiting for this opportunity. When it appears all the bids are in, he posts a bid of maybe $100 more. It looks like he found a great set for maybe half price.

Just then, another bid for $100 more comes in. It seems another buyer had the same idea—the price on these cards is ridiculously cheap, and he has to have them. The first bidder counters

with another offer. Back to the second bidder, who by now is determined to get the cards, because he doesn't know where else he'll
find an unmarred 1962 set. Back and forth it goes; when the dust
settles, the final bid is equal to the original value.

The moral for high-end collectors is: There's always someone
out there who is willing to pay the established value for your cards.

6. UNOPENED MATERIAL.

This is another category limited almost exclusively to dealers
and investors. After all, what collector wouldn't want to open up
boxes to see what he bought?

Dealers often keep a large supply of unopened boxes of recent cards in stock, simply because a good amount of customers
buy exclusively wax box or case material.

A few clarifications of definitions: A WAX PACK is a single,
unopened pack of usually fifteen cards in a wax wrapper. A WAX
BOX is what these packs are put in, usually thirty-six packs to a
simple cardboard box. A CASE is what the wax boxes are shipped
in from the factory or distributor to the dealer; a case usually contains twenty wax boxes. Cards can also be packed in CELLO,
which is short for cellophane wrapping. That's the see-through
plastic that usually holds forty-three cards.

Recently, unopened boxes of cards have become hot collectibles. They've been sold for exorbitant prices. In 1989, one New
York auction house entertained bids for twenty unopened packs of
1952 Bowman football cards. The reserve estimate was listed as
$16,000!

Unopened material—especially older material—appeals almost exclusively to the investor. As stated before, collectors would
rather open the packs to see what cards are in there.

One genre in the unopened material category that is popular
with collectors, however, is the unopened cello. That's because you
can still see the cards at the top and bottom of the packs. In 1989,
cello packs from 1976 and 1977 featuring rookie cards of Walter
Payton and Steve Largent were sold for $500 and $300, respec-

A wax box, wax packs, and cards from 1983 Topps. (Don Butler)

tively. Prices for cellos from 1984 Topps with Eric Dickerson and Dan Marino as the top card brought $100.

Still another genre of unopened material collecting includes wrapper collectors. Limited almost exclusively to collectors and true fans of football cards, wrapper collectors try to collect every type of wrapper ever issued. Condition is the name of the game for wrapper finders. A wrapper is not considered truly mint unless it came straight off the presses, without any folds or creases, or unless the pack has never been opened and is in pristine condition.

Consequently, mint wrappers from early issues are tough to come by. Collecting wrappers is not the same as collecting unopened packs; wrapper collectors are interested only in the wrappers. Though this segment of the hobby is quite small, they are very dedicated and are some of the most knowledgeable collectors around.

7. MASTER SETS.

One subset of collectors which came into vogue after the rise of Pro Set's popularity was "master set" collectors. This meant you tried to collect *everything* issued by Pro Set in a given year—promotional sets, test cards, possibly uncut sheets, and especially the variations.

Master set collecting is especially popular with Pro Set collectors because it's a true challenge. It's easy to go out and buy a complete set from any year. The real joy in master set collecting is looking for those few William Perry cards or those Blair Bush/James Lofton/Thomas Sanders Series II promotional cards, of which only 500 of each were made, and adding them to your set. This boils down to what the hobby is all about. Sure, they're expensive, because they are so rare. But finding one and sliding it into a sleeve with the rest of your Pro Set cards is more than a reward for those days of searching at shows and hours of pouring over hobby classifieds.

Make no mistake: master set collecting is tough, requires long hours, and, these days, is usually expensive. Something allegedly as simple as a 1990 Fleer master set, which would include the Joe Montana yards/touchdowns column headings switch on the back of his card, the four versions of Kevin Butler's card (placekicker or punter on the front; P or PK on the back, in any of the four combinations), the three misnumbered Eagles cards, and the three cards that somehow wound up with a thin black rule between the bio notes and the text, can set you back a total of $100 or more if you're buying from scratch. Some master set collectors also believe the ten 10-card strips given out by Fleer at the 1990 National in Arlington, Texas, should be considered as well. Good luck finding someone with a supply of those.

8. UNCUT SHEETS.

One facet of collecting has been boiled down to the production level—gathering uncut sheets. While this may also come under the heading of master set collecting, those with a yen for a sheet of pre-cut cards also usually have to spend big bucks and make lots of connections before landing sheets. An uncut sheet of cards, in the cases of Score and Topps, means 110 cards on one large piece of cardboard. Because of the unwieldy size, the trouble it takes to store properly, and the difficulty in displaying the sheets, most collectors don't put much value on sheets. If you find a sheet in Very Good or better condition (Mint is a near impossibility, again because of the awkward size), you end up usually paying 60 to 80 percent of the total cost of the cards shown on the sheet.

Uncut sheets are used by football card researchers to clear up some hobby mysteries. In the 1990 Pro Set, Ray Perkins and Johnny Holland variations exist which do not show the man's name and position at the top of the card. Uncut sheets of Pro Set cards, which had two rows of six cards of one player (three-player sheets) were seen with one of the twelve cards missing Holland's or Perkins' name at the top. Since the rest were correct, researchers have no explanation. While these sheets are interesting to look at, the value is usually quite low.

9. COLLECT BY MANUFACTURER.

This seems obvious, but with so many football cards out there, those with limited funds have to pick and choose which cards they want to buy. In this case, many stick with the same brand year after year. Some older collectors may not like Topps' recent direction, but they buy the cards anyway because they have a complete run of Topps football. Younger collectors may buy only the Score or only the Pro Set.

Collecting by manufacturer may also mean collecting anything related to football cards that company has produced. For instance, nobody knows how Pro Set sheets found their way into the hobby, but a master set collector who goes after only Pro Set items—thus making him a one-company collector—will try to find as many uncut sheets as he can to go along with the supplemental sets and variation cards.

Adding all the insert sets and known uncut sheets may also be a priority for a collector who goes after, say, the 1970s Topps material only.

Most people collect sets of cards from wax packs and try to buy single cards to complete older sets. The other genres are considered to be for advanced collectors looking for something different to collect. Until about two years ago, collecting was relatively inexpensive, but now everything in the hobby has quadrupled in price.

(That's one of the reasons master set collecting is limited to a relatively small group of people—if something like the 1990 Pro Set Cody Risien card—which was pulled to make room for Ozzie Newsome but was mysteriously released in wax packs at the end of Series I—actually finds its way onto a dealer's table, you can expect to pay at least $40 for it. Most collectors would rather use the $40 to complete other sets or buy new cards.)

There's an incredible diversity to who and what you can collect in cards. Though most collectors stick to the mainstream nationally released sets, there are enough regional sets, food sets, and supplemental sets out there to pique any collector's interest.

The Odd Man Out

Are they collectible? You've seen them: police sets, food sets, exhibit cards, and special interest cards. These oddball cards have been made for years and are not necessarily johnny-come-latelys.

The earliest of these cards appeared in the late 1940s and early 1950s. Exhibit cards were unnumbered blanked backed, thick stocked, black and white (some were sepia tone) cards measuring $3^1/4'' \times 5^3/8''$.

Price guides attempt to list all the exhibit football cards made during this period. However, there were a number of sets issued and a complete list of all cards issued is difficult to obtain. The top players of the day, both collegiate and professional, were included in the sets.

Also issued in the 1950s were the Bread for Health set, Bazooka cards, the Bell Brad Los Angeles Rams, and the beginning of the Kahn's sets.

Most of the 1950s issues were promotional in nature and most were one shot deals. The Kahn's sets, however, ran from 1959 through 1964. The first two years players from the Cleveland Browns and the Pittsburgh

Phil Simms. Milk carton
collectibles. (Chuck
Bennett)

Steelers made up the sets. They were black and white,
$3^1/4'' \times 3^{15}/16''$ cards with the slogan: Compliments of Kahn's, "The
Wiener The World Awaited". In its third season selected players from
the Baltimore Colts, Los Angeles Rams, and Philadelphia Eagles
were added. In 1962, players from Chicago, Detroit, and Minnesota
were added, while in 1963 six new teams had players represented:
Dallas, Green Bay, New York, St. Louis, San Francisco, and Washington. The 1963 set is also the largest of the sets, numbering ninety-
two. The last set appeared in 1964 when Kahn's issued a full color set
of fifty-three players. Today these sets are quite collectible among
those that can find and afford them.

Because some of these sets were printed in such small quantities
in comparison to the larger manufacturers, scarcity becomes an issue.
Just trying to find some of the cards is a job in itself. Also with the recent boom in football card prices, you can expect that these cards will
draw a nice price tag as well.

In the 1960s these oddball sets became easier to find. The Lake
to Lake Packer set of 1961, the Mayrose Frank St. Louis set of 1960,

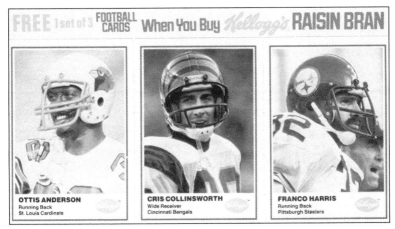

FREE 1 set of 3 FOOTBALL CARDS When You Buy *Kellogg's* RAISIN BRAN

OTTIS ANDERSON
Running Back
St. Louis Cardinals

CRIS COLLINSWORTH
Wide Receiver
Cincinnati Bengals

FRANCO HARRIS
Running Back
Pittsburgh Steelers

(left) Ottis Anderson. (middle) Cris Collinsworth. (right) Franco Harris. Kelloggs. (Chuck Bennett)

the National City Bank Browns set of 1961, the Golden Tulip set of 1961, the Eskimo Pie set of 1969, and the 1968 KDKA Steeler set are all oddball sets. By no means is this a complete list of the sets that appeared during the decade of the 1960s, but rather a highlight of the cards and sets that are available.

Another of the interesting and highly collectible sets of the 1960s is the 1962 Post Cereal set. A set of 200 cards were found on the backs of a number of Post cereal products. The cards had to be cut out by the collector and thus many of the cards that exist today are in poor shape.

Metal coins have made the rounds in in the early 1960s Salada coins were released. A total of 154 make up the set and today a finished set will run you between $2,500 and $3,000.

With the 1970s it seemed that the oddball collectibles became easier to find as companies used football players to promote their products.

Marketing was the new word in business and following the lead of the Post company, Kellogg's introduced three dimensional cards in both 1970 and 1971. Kellogg's also produced similar baseball cards.

Both sets of football cards consist of sixty cards, but the 1971 is

Police Cards issued by local police departments display messages to young card collectors. (Chuck Bennett)

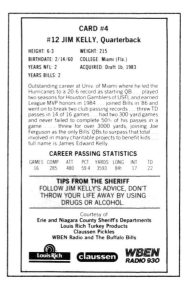

Jim Kelly

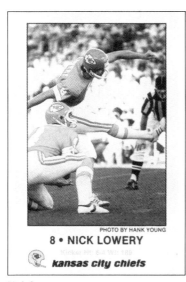

Nick Lowery

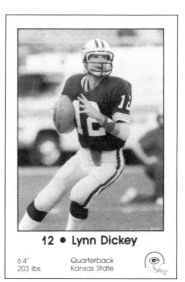

Lynn Dickey

Walter Payton

Louis Lipps   Eric Dickerson

three times more valuable because no box top offer was available. Thus, the only way to get the cards was to buy the cereal.

Coke, Wonder Bread, Slim Jims, and Sunoco all had promotional stamps, caps, cards, and discs but one of the best promotional items was delivered by McDonald's.

In 1975 the McDonald's restaurant chain issued a set of four Quarterback cards with a coupon tabbed on the bottom worth a quarter off a sandwich. Although the set itself is worth only $5 to $10, it set the stage for a mass produced promotional effort between the NFL and the chain that made Ronald McDonald famous later in the 1980s.

The 1976 Crane Disc set is popular with collectors because it features a rookie Walter Payton card or disc.

In or around 1979 the birth of the police cards became a popular way to get a message into the hands of kids. Some of the first police sets were the 1979 Kansas City Chiefs and the 1979 Dallas Cowboys. Since then all twenty-eight NFL teams have had a number of police sets made. The sets vary in terms of value. Some sets, because of limited print runs and the players involved, can be valued at $100 or more, but for the most part police sets tend to be valued in the $5 to $20 range.

Team collectors are big on police sets as are collectors who focus on one or two players. If you are in the area of an NFL franchise you might want to check with the local police public relations staff to see if they will have cards available this coming year.

In 1983 Kellogg's brought back its cards for a brief stint. The 1983 cards are less valuable than the early 1970s ones. The promotion lasted only one year.

In 1985 McDonald's brought back a football card promotional with the Chicago Bears. As the Bears marched through the playoffs and into the Super Bowl, McDonald's was along with different color tabbed cards each week of the four weeks that the promotion ran.

The promotion then found its way into 1986 as McDonald's again released football cards with tabs on the bottom which could be torn off and redeemed for products.

In each of the NFL cities McDonald's gave away cards from the home teams while also having a set of all-star cards for all of the cities that were not near NFL cities. These latter cards are the easiest of the McDonald's cards to find.

While the promotion itself wasn't such a big hit, the effect it had on football card collectors was fantastic. Collectors liked what McDonald's had to offer and quickly ate up the cards.

It was then found out that each week different colored tabbed cards were given out. In week one blue tab cards were given out followed by black, gold, and finally green tabbed cards.

Each set consisted of either twenty-four or twenty-five cards in the team set. Today the cards are still sought by collectors trying to fill sets of all the cards available.

Since 1986 the number of police sets, food issues, and oddball sets in general is substantial. A collector would have to possess vast fortunes and a great deal of luck to be able to collect all that were produced and available to the market.

In 1989 Pacific Trading Cards, Inc., produced a commemorative

Jack Lambert. Mini Poster.
(Chuck Bennett)

set honoring the retiring Steve Largent. The set consists of 110 cards of action and personal photos of Largent. The set takes you from his childhood through his record-setting final season.

Finally, one of the more popular items to collect the past couple of years has been prototype and limited edition cards. In 1988, Pro Set printed an 8-card prototype set and distributed them to dealers and collectors trying to get a feel for how the cards would be accepted. The complete set is rather scarce and is valued at $1000.

A number of companies have printed prototype cards and sent them to the media and to hobby dealers. While these cards are not considered a part of the set, they are deemed valuable by collectors who want cards with short print runs.

At both Super Bowl Card Show I and Super Bowl Card Show II, Score distributed a limited edition card of Franco Harris. Action Packed gave away Prototypes of the 1991 cards at the Super Bowl Card Show II, while Pro Set gave away cards of the show itself. The cards were promotional vehicles for the companies at these large hobby shows. Limited to distribution at these shows only, the value and desire for the cards is dramatically larger than the regular issue cards. Value is very difficult to put on cards with short print runs, nevertheless these limited-edition cards will always stay popular with collectors.

The Rookie Craze

One of the most important trends in the football card collecting hobby during the 1980s was the "Rookie Craze." Once again, the trend occurred in football card collecting after it had hit baseball cards.

In the early 1980s, baseball card collectors saw potential in buying rookie cards. With the simple idea that a player's rookie card would be the first to increase in value if he gains fame, dealers and collectors started a rush on the card's of the top players of the day, especially their rookie cards.

It may have happened a bit later, but football card enthusiasts followed the baseball collector's lead and purchased a number of rookie cards for gridiron stars.

First, let's look at a possible definition of a "rookie card." Most hobby publications define a rookie card as the first regular card of a particular player. This is the player's first appearance on a regular issue card from one of the major card companies (presently Topps, Fleer, Score, Pro Set, Action-Packed, Pacific and Upper Deck). A "major" card issue is one released by a card company on a national basis.

1975 Topps Lynn Swann.
(Chuck Bennett)

Remember, just because a player is playing this season, his rookie card may not be released until next season. When in doubt about a player's rookie card, check one of the price guides. Most price guides have the letters RC next to a player's rookie card.

Another area to be careful with is update cards. Most hobbyists do not consider a player's rookie card to be one included in an update or rookie set. Update sets are found only in hobby shops and are considered "late additions" to the regular set. Yet even though not considered true rookie cards, these "first cards" remain popular.

So why does everyone want rookie cards? Well, those people who are buying up all the rookie cards in sight might not be defined as collectors. They might consider themselves investors or even dealers. It is a fact, however, that rookie cards are among the first off hobby dealer shelves.

Most people seem to think that if a player reaches the level of success of Joe Montana, then his card, too, will rise as did Montana's.

In 1988, you could have purchased a Dalton Hilliard rookie card for just a nickel. That same year you could have obtained Neal An-

1988 Bo Jackson rookie —
value dropped by half
when the seriousness of his
hip injury was revealed.

derson rookie cards for a dime each. Throw in a quarter each for
rookie cards of Vinny Testaverde and Christian Okoye. The high-
priced rookie in 1988 was the Bo Jackson card, which cost in the
neighborhood of $2.

In just two years, each of these players has made a name in the
NFL. While the most expensive card mentioned is the Jackson
rookie, those that bought large quantities of the Hilliard cards have
cashed in as well.

That's it. Buying a card (or number of cards) cheap, guessing
that this player will become a star in the league, and smiling all the
way to the bank as those 5,000 nickel cards turn into $2 gems is thrill-
ing.

But rookie cards are not get-rich schemes. For 1988, (there was
just one company, Topps, in 1988) there are rookie cards for Mike
Tomczak, Ron Rivera, Roger Vick, Floyd Dixon, and Brian
Bosworth.

None of these would have cost much in 1988, except for the
Bosworth card. Remember that in 1988, "The Boz" was the hottest

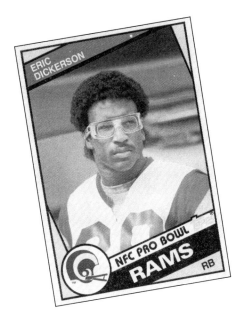

1984 Topps Eric Dickerson,
a NFC Pro Bowler. (Chuck
Bennett)

thing going in sports. His face was on every major magazine and the public was intrigued by this cult hero.

Be sure that some dealer, and maybe many in the Seattle area, bought up plenty of Bosworth cards. Investors reached deep into their pockets only to find the card now on a steady downward spiral that won't stop until he's back among the ranks of the commons. So, if you bought 100 Bosworth rookies when they were hot (in the $1 to $2 range), today you would have some expensive commons. Be careful.

If for the most part rookies are good buys, are there any guidelines to investing?

Here are a few basic rules to remember. Cards are for fun; collecting cards can be enjoyed by all. If you want to invest in a card lot of 100 of your favorite players, that's okay, just don't go too deep. We don't recommend buying large quantities because the players are unproven.

In 1987, Tim Brown came out of Notre Dame as college foot-

1988 Topps Neal Anderson

ball's best player and his card value has climbed as high as his jersey number. In 1984, there was Doug Flutie and in 1983 Mike Rozier. Both Flutie and Rozier's rookie cards fell in the USFL sets, but neither demand much attention or money because neither did much in the NFL.

Second, stick with offensive players in the skill positions. Quarterbacks and running backs are the best bets to make it for rookie cards. Ever since the days of Bronko Nagurski, quarterbacks have been the media darlings of the league. During the next Super Bowl, watch how many visits the quarterbacks and running backs get. Receivers are the next best investment.

This is not to say that the defensive dominators of the game aren't worth your time. Fewer linebackers and lineman can dominate a game like somebody with the ball. Lawrence Taylor, however, is one of those defensive players.

Still, for you to invest in rookie cards, you'll need to get to them early while they are still cheap. In the case of defensive players, it may

1982 Topps Ronnie Lott, a
NFC All Pro player. (Chuck
Bennett)

take time to know if you have a winner. The Tampa Bay Bucs chose
Keith McCants as the third player in the draft in 1990, yet he didn't
start until the last few games of the season.

And finally, keep up with current stats, records, and general
news. We were thrilled to watch as 1990 Rookie of the Year Emmitt
Smith of the Dallas Cowboys broke loose for 147 yards and 2 touchdowns during a 1990 Thanksgiving Day victory over archrival Washington Redskins. Keep up with your favorites, wait patiently as they
develop and grab their cards before there's a big rush.

When a player outdistances himself from the rest of the pack
and is headed for greatness, then the margin of profit rises and the
margin of chance decreases. Early in 1989, Barry Sanders was just
another Heisman winner who had yet to prove his value. Many experts said he was too small to become a big time player in the NFL.
Many collectors thought that he would get stuck in Detroit without
any publicity and on a losing team.

The Lions didn't win many in 1989, but Sanders won plenty of fans. The overachiever broke on the scene about halfway through the year and easily ran away with Rookie of the Year honors.

His rookie cards (1989 Score #257 and 1989 Pro Set #494) jumped up as quickly as any card in the past decade, making collectors and investors scramble to find a good buy. Today, Sanders' rookie cards look like solid investments and great cards to collect.

Position Importance

Here's a classic example of the differences in values of football cards.

Two outstanding rookies came out of the 1966 Philadelphia football set—Dick Butkus and Gale Sayers. Sayers, though his career was drastically shortened by a knee injury, turned out to be one of the most exciting players of the 1960s and early 1970s. Butkus is the man many believe was the greatest middle linebacker ever, and was one of the greatest competitors the game has ever seen. After his retirement, Sayers wrote a couple of excellent books and has kept a low profile. Butkus, on the other hand, has appeared in numerous TV commercials, had bit parts in movies, and was an analyst for CBS's NFL telecasts.

Based on that information, you would assume the two rookie cards are comparable in price or that the rookie card of Butkus, with his recent TV exposure, might even be worth a little more than Sayers' card. But the Sayers card is worth about $100 more than the Butkus card.

Why? The bottom line is the importance collectors have placed on the player's position.

There are two rules of thumb to remember: offense is ALWAYS worth more than defense, and quarterbacks, running backs, and wide receivers draw the most attention.

Some of the most valuable football cards of the last thirty years include the Joe Namath rookie, Walter Payton rookie, Steve Largent rookie, second year cards for all three, Gale Sayers rookie, and Joe Montana rookie cards.

Notice that each of the three is either a quarterback, running back or wide receiver. If you're looking to put some money into a card of just one player, go after somebody such as Barry Sanders, Troy Aikman, Dan Marino, Art Monk, or Jerry Rice. Because their statistics are measured so easily, and because the television camera is on them so often, these players are the sure bets to see rising card prices. Their cards will always be valuable to somebody. These cards are the superstars, the Jack Nicholsons of the football card hobby.

The ones with values that are toughest to gauge are offensive lineman. The cliche is you never hear about them unless they catch a

1971 Topps Bobby Bell. This year's hot rookie cards can cost five times as much as this HOFer. (Don Butler)

pass or are flagged for a holding penalty. Can you name even one of-fensive lineman who made the Pro Bowl last year?

More than in any other sport, a player's position in football deter-mines his card value. With that in mind, here's a position-by-position comparison of relative card values, using the 1990 football cards as a guideline. Positions are ranked in order of card value.

1. QUARTERBACK.

At the beginning of the 1990 collecting season—June—the high-profile draft picks were the highest priced cards, meaning col-lectors were seeking out these cards and driving up the value. In-cluded in that half-dozen were two quarterbacks, Jeff George and Andre Ware. Rounding out the top fifteen most valuable 1990 cards at the season's onset were Joe Montana, Jim Everett, and Dan Marino, plus second-year cards of Bubby Brister, Chris Miller, Don Majkowski, and Troy Aikman.

Most starting NFL quarterbacks go for at least twenty cents in

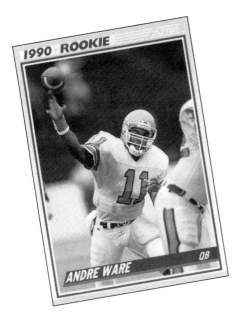

Andre Ware — though he had yet to play an NFL down, he had some of the highest priced cards of 1990. (Don Butler)

new card issues, and starting QBs are generally a good buy. Dave Krieg, who has been maligned for years but statistically has proven to be an excellent passer (believe it or not, through 1989, Krieg was ranked fourth on the all-time quarterback rating scale), finally had his cards begin to move upward in value in 1990.

Of course, if you were one of the few who actually had several 1981 and 1982 Joe Montana cards, you know his rookie card went from $10 to $50 to $175 to $200-plus, with excellent chances of increasing still further as he continues to lead San Francisco to Super Bowls and pull out victories in the last two minutes. Quarterbacks who become stars, then potential Hall of Famers, have consistently proven to show the most growth in the value of their cards.

Two other good examples are Don Majkowski and Troy Aikman. Both had rookie cards in the 1989 Score set. Majkowski's card started with a value of about $1, while Aikman's was about twice that. But when Majkowski led the Packers to the brink of the playoffs and found himself named a Pro Bowl quarterback, collectors realized he was a star and pushed his cards up to $3.50. Aikman, though he took a pounding his first year in Dallas, really didn't look too bad. He was, after all, drafted number one. His cards moved up in value a little. In 1990, collectors realized Majkowski was the man who made the Packers go. Yes, a superstar. Tack another $2 to $4 on the price of that card. When a shoulder injury prematurely ended his season, his cards leveled out at the $5 to $6 mark. Down in Cowboy country, Aikman was helping Dallas to flirt with .500 and a playoff spot through most of the season. A superstar in the making. Aikman's 1990 Score card rocketed to $10.

Another recent mover is Dan Marino's 1984 rookie card, which rose from $15 to $30 in the space of about five months in 1990. When you look and see a player is the second- or third-best all-time passer (as Marino is), it's a good idea to find as many rookie cards as you can while they're still low.

Since quarterbacks have the highest profile on and off the field, it's very difficult to keep the secret of a good buy. Old-time players such as John Brodie and Chuck Conerly, neither of whom are in the Hall of Fame, command sometimes twice as much as any Hall of Fame defensive player from the same era. Recently, rookie and second-year cards of HOFers Len Dawson and Sonny Jurgenson have begun to climb the $100-plus ladder in value as high-end collectors search out the few good buys left at quarterback.

Quarterbacks, then, will on average always be the highest-priced cards of any new issue because of their high profile and importance to the team. They've also shown the most growth when a player becomes a superstar and a Hall of Fame prospect.

2. RUNNING BACK.

In the football card world, the other impact rookies in the 1990 card sets were running backs, another high-profile position. Fleer was the first company out with a Blair Thomas card, and pricing began at $1.25 and remained there most of the collecting season. Thomas' Score release went for around $1; Pro Set's Thomas issue in Series II went for a little under $1; and his Topps card also went for around $1. Finding doubles of Blair Thomas was

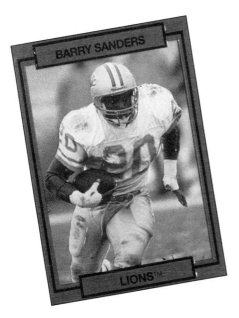

1990 Action Packed Barry Sanders — a second year card with lots of potential. (Don Butler)

1989 Score's Thurman Thomas rookie rose from less than $5 to $15 when Buffalo made Super Bowl XXV. (Don Butler)

a boon to any collector opening a wax pack, but he wasn't the only $1-plus running back in 1990.

Barry Sanders, the hottest rookie of 1989, also started at $1 in most 1990 issues and remained at that level, or rose slightly in value toward $1.50, despite a mediocre start. (Sanders didn't have a 100-yard game until halfway through the season.) When he finally got going and became tenth player to have back-to-back 1,000-yard seasons his first two years in the league, the value of his second card began to move. Compared to the $30 value of his 1989 Score rookie card, there was much more room for growth in his second-year cards. Any of his cards—especially his Fleer issue, believed to be the scarcest of the four easily available sets—is destined to rise at least another $3 or $4 during the next few years to keep pace with his rookie card. That is dependent, of course, on Sanders continuing to have a standout career.

Thurman Thomas was a late bloomer for card collectors. Before the 1990 playoffs, his 1989 Score rookie card sold well at $3.50 each. (For the second straight year, he was among the NFL leaders in rushing and all-purpose yardage.) When the Bills destroyed Miami and the Raiders en route to Super Bowl XXV, his cards shot up to more than $10 within three weeks. That makes his card the second most valuable of the set.

Two-sport superstar Bo Jackson was another running back who started out at $1 or more in each of his 1990 card values. His popularity among younger collectors is what drove his 1989 Score update card (showing a Nike photo of him in pads and a bat over his shoulders) to more than $20. With his hip injury, the value of his cards has dropped. Though still somewhat popular, his cards will never have the $1-plus impact they had in 1989 and 1990.

Rounding out the high-priced new issues were any of the early 1990 picks—Atlanta's Steve Broussard, Rodney Hampton of the Giants, San Francisco's Dexter Carter, Green Bay's Darrell Thompson, and Phoenix back Anthony Thompson. Each of these rookies began 1990 valued at fifty cents or more weeks before the season even opened, and none of them were guaranteed a great amount of playing time.

Newcomers Emmitt Smith and Johnny Johnson out shone them all by the end of 1990, however. By the end of the season, Smith's cards were around $3, while Johnson's were at $2.

Veteran and second-year backs at twenty cents or more in early 1990 cards included Herschel Walker, Neal Anderson, Christian Okoye, and the second-year cards of Bobby Humphrey, Sammie Smith, Eric Metcalf, and Dave Meggett. On a level just below that are such surprises as Roger Craig, Dalton Hillard, Thurman Thomas, and Greg Bell. By 1991, Thomas, Humphrey, Anderson, and Meggett were each at a thirty-five cent level.

3. WIDE RECEIVER.

The only flanker to start at seventy-five cents in 1990 was everybody's all-time superstar, Jerry Rice. It's a given that any new Rice card will start at fifty cents. As the years go by, though, these later releases won't show nearly as much gain as his first three cards from Topps. Still, if you're short on money and want to buy a wide receiver's card that will rise in value, pick up any Rice card.

The forty-cent level belonged to second-year cards of Sterling Sharpe and John Taylor. It's too early to tell if these two will be sure bets; Taylor will be twenty-nine in 1991 and was injured early in his career, and while Green Bay's offense has come alive under Majkowski and Sharpe, it's still sporadic. Both Sharpe and Taylor have proven to be outstanding athletes with great hands. Another second-year player, Flipper Anderson of the Rams, went for around thirty cents.

Oddly, Andre Rison's 1990 second-year cards started at twenty-five cents and moved to maybe forty cents even though he was leading the league in receiving much of the year. Most of the attention went to his 1989 Score rookie card, but his second-year card should've drawn some attention.

Other receivers who started at the fifteen- to twenty-cent level are Anthony Carter, Al Toon, Art Monk, and Brian Blades.

4. LINEBACKER.

Mike Singletary, Lawrence Taylor, Karl Mecklenburg, and Derrick Thomas are instantly recognizable to any card collector. The decade of the 1980s again saw the rise of the linebacker as a

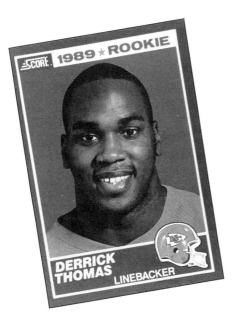

1989 Score's Derrick Thomas — the first linebacker to break the $5 mark his second year in the league. (Don Butler)

glamor position, thanks to Lawrence Taylor. The position's other big decade was the 1960s, when men such as Sam Huff, Dick Butkus, and Ray Nitschke roamed the middle.

With young players such as Tim Harris, Derrick Thomas and Chris Spielman making the Pro Bowl, it seems the 1990s will be another big decade for linebackers. Since it's difficult to figure out what rookie is having an impact and which young player will push a veteran out of a job, most linebacker cards start low and don't really begin to pick up until after the season, when the Pro Bowlers are announced and season-ending rankings appear. Linebacker is one of the juiciest areas for collectors with an eye on future sales, since these cards show more movement than any other defensive position. Cards of stars such as Taylor, Singletary, Mecklenburg, and Harris all commanded a nickel or more above common prices in 1990, not bad considering Singletary and Taylor are sure-shot HOFers, Mecklenburg is close, and Harris is a rising star.

5. TIGHT END.

Tight ends are generally common cards, since the player is usually called upon to block more than to catch. Blocking holds no value for today's card collectors, so unless the player is a rarity such as Ozzie Newsome, this is a position to stay clear of. Consider that of the 150-plus players in the Hall of Fame, exactly one is a tight end—Mike Ditka.

Ozzie Newsome is a lock for the Hall of Fame, and John Mackey will one day be inducted as well. Still, Newsome's 1990 cards rarely sold for more than a dime. In 1990, only a few tight end cards were valued at more than a nickel to start the season— Newsome, the Bengals' Rodney Holman, and the Eagles' young superstar Keith Jackson, whose cards were at twenty cents.

6. SAFETY/CORNERBACK.

Again, it's tough to name any Pro Bowl players outside Ronnie Lott at this position. Recent card crops have not been good for the safeties and corners—we're sure there's some mathematical equation to measure the impact of a cover man and the men who burn him and his card values, but the end result is an undervalued card.

Newcomers such as Brian Blades, Tim McDonald, and Erik McMillan may make this a position to watch in the 1990s. Rookie cards for all three are at least sixty cents apiece (cards are from 1988 to 1989). Their 1990 issues, however, were only a nickel or so above common prices at best.

7. DEFENSIVE LINE.

This is another weak position because linemen just aren't considered collectible. Only Keith Millard of the Vikings, Bruce Smith of the Bills, Reggie White the Eagles, Howie Long of the Raiders, and Richard Dent of the Bears were valued at more than seven cents in any 1990 release, while such all-pros as Charles Haley, Chris Doleman, Andre Tippett, Leslie O'Neal, and Lee Williams were a nickel or less. Now that most teams have moved away from the 4-3 defense, the emphasis on sacks—one of the few measurable statistics for a defensive player—has gone to the linebackers. Even when a tough DE such as Dent does come along, he usually gets double-teamed by the offensive line, so sacks and tackles again go to the blitzing linebackers.

Even when the card boom took off, such players as Merlin Olsen, Bob Lilly, Deacon Jones, and Randy White went overlooked while prices on linebackers and safeties went up. Unless a truly dynamic player comes along, there probably won't be too much collector interest in this position. The glamor position on defense will always belong to the linebackers.

8. SPECIALISTS (KICKERS/PUNTERS).

A lot of young collectors/investors make the mistake of picking up rookie cards of kickers simply because they score a lot of points. Would you believe thirty cents for a David Treadwell rookie card?

Of all the positions, rookie cards of placekickers rise the quickest and fall the quickest. Stay away from these cards, because the chances of a kicker's card retaining value is virtually nil.

Again, look at the Hall of Fame credentials. Most of the HOF kickers doubled as something else—George Blanda at quarterback, Paul Hornung as tailback, Lou Groza as linebacker.

Today's kickers are purely specialists. Since the 1960s, when the position became specialized and soccer-style kickers came into vogue, only a few notable players have held card values: Green Bay's Don Chandler, Minnesota's Fred Cox, Miami's Garo Yepremian, and Kansas City's Jan Stenerud. Chandler, Cox, and Yepremian were high-profile players who played integral parts in their teams' dynasties for years. There is no kicker today about whom that can be said; even San Francisco has had turnover in the kicking department, from Ray Wersching to Mike Cofer.

Stenerud lasted for more than fifteen years, is the second leading scorer of all time, and was the first pure kicker to make the Hall of Fame when he was a first-ballot inductee in 1991. He is the exception. Kickers today generally last about five years. A few, such as Eddie Murray, Chris Bahr and Nick Lowery, have already lasted longer, but their rookie cards don't even clear fifty cents.

When the mania for those wonderful 1984 Topps cards hit in 1989, the rookie card for Giants' kicker Ali Hadji-Shiekh rose to $2 in some areas. Now, you should be able to pick it up at common price, as he's no longer in the league.

Of the specialists, kickers are far more valuable (remember, though, value is a relative term here) than punters. The only punter to really have an impact on the football card hobby is future Hall of Famer Ray Guy; you can find his 1974 rookie cards usually for less than $4. Guy is an obvious exception to the Hall of Fame derby—a true specialist who was spectacular at his position for more than ten years. The only other punters you'll find in the Hall of Fame were two-way players such as Yale Lary, who also played safety for the 1950s Detroit Lions. Since Guy was "only" a punter, all of his cards are extremely undervalued when compared to other potential Hall of Famers.

In 1990, most kickers were considered commons, though a few—Treadwell, Green Bay's Chris Jacke, Chicago's Kevin Butler—were a nickel or seven cents.

Stay away from kicker cards.

9. OFFENSIVE LINEMEN.

You want card obscurity? You can go no lower than an offensive lineman. Even defensive linemen have some statistics on which a card collector can make a choice whether or not to buy a card in quantity. The only statistics the offensive linemen have are games played and penalties.

Sure, in the macho game of football there are no tougher players. Somebody like Chris Hinton could take a David Treadwell and his higher-priced cards and use him to pick dirt off his face mask. Unfortunately, kickers and even punters get more air time with one minute's worth of work per game than a lineman gets in thirty minutes.

Linemen are underrated because they do their job in obscurity until, as stated before, they're caught for holding. The wise card buyer will watch the Pro Bowl rosters, read his programs and media guides, and keep close watch on the text of his card backs to pick his 100-card lots, since most linemen (Tony Mandarich excepted) start their card careers as commons. If a guy makes a fourth or fifth straight Pro Bowl and is in his very early thirties, start looking for his rookie card. This means players such as Chris Hinton, Jay Hilgenberg, and Jackie Slater, to name three.

You won't know it until their careers have been over five years, but once they are elected into the Hall of Fame, the effect on their cards is enormous.

The most classic example of this is Bob St. Clair, who was elected in 1990. His cards were always listed as commons, but once he was chosen, his $3.50 1957 rookie cards soared to the $25 mark.

Of the current players, Anthony Munoz, a nine-time Pro Bowler, is a lock for the Hall of Fame. Even so, his rookie cards from 1982 are still a good buy at under $6. His subsequent cards are barely above common price.

The only problem with rookie cards of offensive linemen is they're usually the only linemen cards to have much value. Subsequent cards of linemen, such as Forrest Gregg, Jim Parker and Jim Ringo, still don't sell for more than $7—maybe double the price of a common card from the late 1950s to mid-1960s.

With a little research, this is a position that can make you money in the long run, but you have to watch for good deals on rookie cards. In 1990, only Tony Mandarich, Munoz and any member of the 1990 rookie crop garnered more than a common price and by the end of the season, prices for all rookie linemen, except Pro Bowler Richmond Webb, dropped to around the common price. There are deals to be found, but you may have to wait awhile to see if your buys pay off.

As the popularity of a player depends largely on his position, so does the value of his cards. When buying large quantities of cards, stay away from the kickers and offensive linemen; try to get the quarterbacks, running backs and wide receivers as early as you can when the new cards come out so you won't be stuck having to pay higher prices a few months later.

To Err Is Human, to Variate Is Collectible

Some of the most interesting developments—in fact, one of the keys to the recent success of football cards—involves errors and variations, one of the most controversial trends in card hobby history.

A variation occurs any time a card company finds an error on a card and corrects it by releasing the same card with different information or a different photo. A variation can be as major as running the wrong photo of a player or as minor as a slight cropping difference in the photo.

As mentioned before, errors and variations played a big part in the establishment of the 1989 football card boom. When Pro Set was first released, the company immediately established itself, and the tone of that particular collecting season, by releasing an unauthorized William Perry card. Perry at the time was not under contract with the NFL Players Association, which licensed cards to Pro Set; therefore, no further cards could be issued. As many as 10,000 were released in early Pro Set wax boxes. When collectors realized how scarce they were, there were near stampedes to hobby stores and retail chains to buy up all the Pro Set they could find in search of the card. Within two weeks, the value of the card rose from $60 to $100, which shows you what kind of demand there was for Pro Set cards in May and June of 1989.

The master set collector came to Pro Set soon after. As explained earlier, a master set collection is one which contains every card printed by a company for a particular season—no matter how scarce the card is. Master setters would soon find how difficult it would be to complete a 1989 master Pro Set. It looked pretty easy at first: just the Perry card plus an eight-card test set that was issued in Arizona.

Soon after, it was discovered that Pro Set made several other early adjustments on a few of its cards. John Elway's card #100 originally read, "Drafted 1st Round, '83," which was corrected to "Acquired trade, '83." The total number of rushing yards originally given for Curt Warner in the text on the back of his card #404 was 1,455; that was corrected to 6,074. And the most miniscule error of all for this particular correction run was on Anthony Miller's card #363. The uncorrected touchdown total in the last statistical column read 14.8. It was upgraded to 3.

Big deal, you say. That's what everybody said. But in the variation crazed summer of 1989, when everyone corrected wrong photos and information on baseball cards, it was a major deal for a football company to actually admit to making errors, then saying it would correct them. Pro Set's philosophy was "the living card set," which meant it would correct errors and update its cards at the beginning, middle, and end of the season.

Until 1989, there had been relatively few variations in football cards; by December 1989, master set finders would have to add some thirty additional cards to their 1989 Pro Set issue, not including a horde of supplemental cards.

First, a couple of definitions. A prototype set or test set is exactly as the term implies—it's a chance for a company to work out potential design or printing problems. A limited number of these cards are made and are usually kept within company walls; thus the public never sees them. The reason they're valuable is because the print run is very limited, they usually feature stars, and because the design is always changed on the final product.

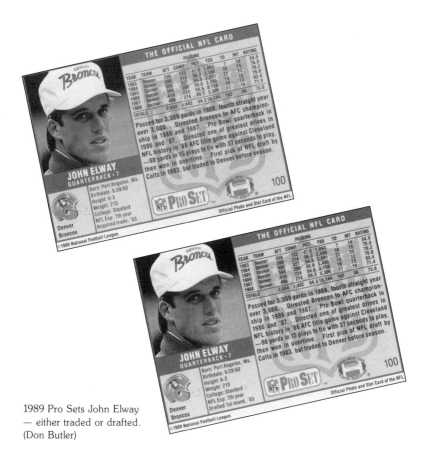

1989 Pro Sets John Elway
— either traded or drafted.
(Don Butler)

A pair of "Leroy Kelly" prototype cards from Topps circa the early 1970s (it's thought they might even be from the 1970 season) surfaced in a late 1990 auction by noted dealer Alan "Mr. Mint" Rosen. The cards featured a pair of radically different designs, neither of which turned up on a regular issue Topps card. Nobody knows how they got out of Topps' vault, but several insiders have said Topps has issued "house" versions of all its sportscards to be circulated only among employees throughout the 1970s.

The first 1989 test set Pro Set made showcased eight players— Dan Marino, Jerry Rice, Eric Dickerson, Reggie White, Mike Singletary, Frank Minnifield, Phil Simms, and Jim Kelly. Fronts were very similar to the 1989 Pro Set release, but backs were horizontal instead

Jim Kelly's 1989 Pro Set
"test set" card. (Don
Butler)

of vertical. It's interesting to note that of all the photos used on the eight-card test set, only Jerry Rice's was carried over to the regular issue. About 2,500 test sets were made, and many were given away at a 1989 candy show in Phoenix, Arizona, where Pro Set was showing its new product to wholesalers. When Pro Set caught fire, the set moved up in value from $150 to $500.

Moving ahead to Pro Set's second test set from early 1990, the Randall Cunningham set features the same photo on all five cards but shows Pro Set experimented with different borders and different placement of the Pro Set logo. The back of each test card is exactly the same, and matches the 1989 Pro Set regular issue Randall Cunningham card. Pro Set President Lud Denny hung on to most of the Cunningham test sets, but several have leaked into the hobby. It's thought that no more than fifty exist. The few that have found their way to the hobby have been sold by dealers for $700 or more.

Pro Set continued to make corrections throughout its 1989 Series I release. Pro Set continued its philosophy in its Series II released in September 1989. Blue traded stripes were added to the cards of

Dan Marino's 1989 Pro Set
"test set" card. (Don
Butler)

players who warranted it and the Series I miscues, which were also
re-released with the Series II cards were corrected.

All this led to a lot of confusion for longtime collectors, but younger collectors loved it and Pro Set sales boomed. Pro Set's "we find
an error, we'll correct it" philosophy created a dilemma for collectors
and price guide coordinators—how do you determine when an error
is turned into a variation and find out its scarcity? Answer—you
guess. Pro Set made no announcement on its corrections; the company left it to sharp-eyed collectors and dealers to find them.

Variations from the 1989 set still seem to crop up. It wasn't until
May 1990 that another scarce nationally issued Pro Set variation was
found. Gizmo Williams card #535 of the 1989 set already received
one correction when a "scouting photo" tagline was added. But a
California collector noticed something odd about one of his non-
scouting photo card backs—there was a misspelling that seemed to
be corrected in other Gizmo Williams cards that also lacked the scouting photo legend. The first line of text mentions the Canadian Football League in the first line of type, but it's spelled "Canadian Footbal"

instead. If you examine the subsequent correction closely, it appears a second "I" was put in by hand, perhaps just before the rest of the sheets were printed. When word finally got out there may be another variation in 1989 Series II Pro Set, the value of the "Canadian Footbal" Gizmo Williams card rose from $20 to $35 to $150. It's estimated that 5,000 exist today, but the prices on all the variations have dropped off.

In September 1990, another variation was found on Jim McMahon's #478 card—when the traded stripe was added, so was a small blurb in italic type that read, "See Bears card 44." Some of the earliest traded McMahons didn't get the "See Bears" sentence added, however. Two months later, the same find was made on a Gerald Riggs card with the blue traded stripe—the back of the card was missing the "See Falcons card 14" line at the bottom of the text that was added to the rest of the traded Riggs cards. The same thing occurred on the Earnest Byner card as well. Since fewer than ten cards with the traded stripe and missing the italic type on the back have been found on each of the three, any of these would definitely be the rarest 1989 Pro Set variations.

The incredible popularity of the Pro Set test sets with collectors began an entire new wave in card manufacturing—that of producing limited promotional sheets of cards and individual card samples to give to collectors at shows. Three more ultra-scarce Pro Set cards appeared at card shows in San Francisco and Chicago in the fall of 1989. Pro Set was preparing the release of its Series II cards and brought along some samples to hand out. Included were three cards that were pulled from the series even before the cards were released—Blair Bush, James Lofton, and Thomas Sanders. The three were replaced, in no particular order, by William Perry, Eric Dickerson and Billy Joe Tolliver, although Thomas Sanders received a card—but on a different number. Fewer than 500 each of the cards are thought to exist. Each is valued at $200 or more.

Most collectors anticipated more of the same out of Pro Set at the end of the year, and they weren't disappointed. The first unusual card Pro Set came up with was a Santa Claus card given out to dealers in December 1989. The card showed a picture of Santa in an array of NFL attire sitting at a table and holding up a Pro Set card. In the background you can see two elves peeking through the window—NFL Properties' John Bello and Pro Set President Lud Denny. When the collecting public got wind of this card (about 5,000 were printed), demand pushed the price to the $100 to $150 level.

In January 1990, Pro Set created a prototype card of the 1989 Rookie of the Year, Barry Sanders. (Pro Set is now the sponsor of the NFL's Rookie of the Year award.) The card, of which about 1,000 were produced, turned out to be different than the regular issue Barry Sanders Rookie of the Year card. The prototype was given to some dealers at a Super Bowl card show and to dealers at a card show in Hawaii in February; when the regular issue was released three months later and turned out to be different, the prototype began selling at $50 to $100.

On Draft Day 1990, Pro Set created more difficult to find cards. At the draft, Pro Set wanted to give the number one choice a card of him with the team that picked him. Since Pro Set didn't know who the pick would be, but could make some educated guesses, four cards were made—three showing Jeff George either with the Falcons, Colts or Patriots, and one showing Keith McCants with the Falcons. More than 2,000 of each were printed, just to cover tracks. After some wheeling and dealing, the Colts ended up with the first pick and chose quarterback Jeff George. Pro Set officials immediately showed up with its Jeff George/Colts cards, and had him pose with a handful. George was then given a few hundred of his Colts card.

But what happened to the rest of the unused George Patriots/ Falcons cards and the Keith McCants card? Some were stolen from the Draft Day studio in New York. Many of the other four-card sets began making the hobby rounds in the summer of 1990. Going price for a set of the four Draft Day cards was $300, and the sheer number that appeared just four months after the draft leads some to believe that as many as 7,000 to 10,000 sets were actually made.

Would variations appear in the 1990 Pro Set as anticipated? You didn't even have to wait until the opening of the season to find out. Denny told *Sports Collectors Digest*, a weekly hobby publication, that three cards had already been corrected in the 1990 set a month before it was even on the shelves. The cards were to be corrected after 7,000 of each of the uncorrected cards were issued in the first print run. Chris Hinton and Andre Rison, both of whom went to Atlanta in that draft day deal for the rights to Jeff George, were to receive blue traded stripes on their cards. Earl Ferrell, who violated the NFL's drug use policy and was kicked out of the league for a year, would receive a blue "retired" stripe, Denny said.

Just to show how quick plans change, the only card of the three that was actually released with the stripe was the Chris Hinton card. But twenty-five other errors were spotted and corrected in the 1990 Series I batch.

Two errors of a different sort stirred the hobby for Pro Set in 1990. Card #338 was originally supposed to be the Pro Bowl card of Eric Dickerson. But Dickerson was another NFLPA holdout who couldn't be used in the set until an agreement could be reached. Pro Set had already made hundreds of thousands of the Dickerson cards and had to hand-pull them from the early 1990 cases. As you might guess, some 500 to 1,000 were released to cases sent to East Coast dealers. The card soared to more than $100 almost overnight, and outrageous sales for the card were reported—one collector traded his collection of 1986-87 Fleer basketball cards, a set valued at nearly $700, for the Dickerson card. The value of the card continued to drop as Pro Set officials told the hobby that *when* an agreement with Dickerson was reached, the card *would be* available from Pro Set for free.

As surely as Jerry Rice will make the Hall of Fame, another card pulled from the set mysteriously began turning up—this time for different reasons. While Pro Set was beginning to print its cards in the early part of 1990, offensive lineman Cody Risien announced he had retired from the Browns. Pro Set decided to pull card #75, Cody Risien, in order to include Ozzie Newsome. It turns out Pro Set had sent a few of the cards as samples with the Spring 1990 Pro Set Gazette to some collectors; others hobbyists scratched their heads when they found the "new" #75 in late Series I wax packs, only to be delighted when they discovered it carried a value of more than $100. It's believed that at least 5,000 were released to the public, and there are no explanations as to why the Risien card began turning up in late-run wax. Did Pro Set run out of Newsome cards? Were the Risiens simply overlooked in the last few Series I sheets to be cut and collated? Who knows? But the Risien card, like the Dickerson card, began to fall out of favor with collectors as more and more were found and the value dropped to $35 to $50.

Let's not forget the other companies during this period either. Most did release some variations with little fanfare and usually little interest. In its initial 1989 set, Score quietly corrected nine errors (including several wrong photos and several cards where the player's jersey did not match up with the number listed on the back) in its late-run wax and factory sets. Most collectors were content with finding either card because finding any type of Score football card became difficult. The much scarcer corrected versions command upward of $4—if you can find them. (A list appears at the end of this chapter.)

In that crazy year of 1989, even Topps had variations—however, they're blamed on a faulty printing process and command no premium value. On Rodney Holman's card #32, six different versions of the word "Bengals" have been detected. One has a small space between the B and the E. A second shows the B slightly above the rest of the line of type. The third has the B a bit below the line of type. The fourth shows just the B with no letters behind it. The fifth has the B partially superimposed over the E. The final version is the easiest to find, as it's the corrected version. It's believed the line of type with "Bengals" fell off the printing plate and had to be replaced several times.

Moving ahead to 1990, Pro Set was again the leader in variations, with newcomer Fleer a surprising second—surprising because Fleer officials had made several statements to the hobby to the effect that errors would not be corrected. Well, Fleer cards hadn't been out more than a month when the first variation turned up on the card of no less of a player than Joe Montana. On his #10 card back, the touchdown and yards headings are reversed in the error issues. The scarcer error card peaked at a value of about $20 before dropping to the $10 mark.

Probably the oddest Fleer issues of all were two misnumbered cards in the middle of the Philadelphia Eagles team set. When Fleer originally drew up its checklist, it was for some reason unable to include quarterback Randall Cunningham (it's thought he, like Dickerson, wouldn't sign with NFL Properties, but either did sign or reached individual agreements with the card companies). When the set was

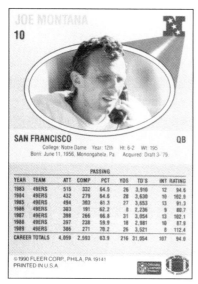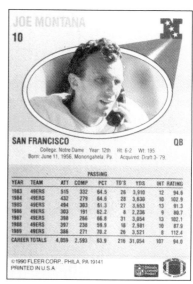

1990 Fleer's Joe Montana variation shows the uncorrected and corrected "TD's" and "YDs" switch. (Don Butler)

first released, the original numbering went like this: 81 Chris Carter, 82 Byron Evans, 84 Ron Heller, 84 Terry Hoage, 85 Wes Hopkins. Sure enough, Cunningham signed a contract with the NFLPA and Fleer was allowed to include him in the set. To maintain the alphabetical continuity, Fleer put Cunningham on card 82 and was supposed to move Evans and Heller up to cards 83 and 84, respectively, while dropping Hoage from the set. When the cards came out, though, Evans and Heller still were at 82 and 83—two #82s and an 83, but no 84. Fleer eventually corrected the numbering.

Even Topps, notorious for not correcting miscues, got into the act. The entire 1990 set came in two varieties. On the back of the first, cards read, "Topps football player cards are not manufactured, sponsored or authorized by any team or league." Topps printed the cards before it had a contract with NFL Properties; after an agreement was reached, cards were reissued with the NFL logo.

It must be emphasized here that an error will not command more than "normal" card price unless the card has been corrected.

Since every card has been printed in equal amounts, a simple uncorrected error will be found in the same quantities as other cards—no more, no less. If it's a notorious error, it may draw initial attention, but most collectors don't buy errors for the sake of buying errors. A corrected card means, of course, there are two different versions of the card. That immediately signifies to collectors one of the versions is scarcer than the other. If an error is found early in a print run and corrected, the error version will be worth more because it's scarcer. If a card isn't corrected until late in the print run, the corrected version will be more expensive because it's scarcer. If you plan on jumping into variations with both feet, make sure you check price guides to find which version is scarcer. Remember, though, investing in variations is risky. When interest dims, variation card values drop quickly.

We've taken a look at some of the most notorious variations of the past few years. They aren't the only variations, though.

ERRORS AND VARIATIONS OVER THE YEARS

While it may seem that 1989 was the Year of the Variation, its history actually goes back quite a few years. Probably the most notorious involves two cases as diverse as a Supreme Court justice and a football Hall of Famer.

In 1955, Topps' All-American set of 100 cards included an issue of Byron "Whizzer" White. In one of the first football wrongback incidents on record, many of the cards had backs that were switched with Gaynell Tinsley. Though it now appears that a lot of the cards in the set had switched backs, the Whizzer White/ Gaynell Tinsley issue was common enough to merit full "variation" listing. (A wrongback—the front of the card shows one player, the back has the back of another card—is considered a printing mistake and is not considered a variation unless a good percentage turn up.)

The most famous football card error though, involves the Green Bay Packer fullback and Hall of Famer Jim Taylor and occurred over a period of three years. His rookie card in 1959 depicted not the burly, crewcutted fullback, but a burly, crewcutted linebacker by the name of Jim Taylor who played for the St. Louis Cardinals. Apparently nobody noticed it the first time, or if they did, they simply snickered to themselves. Unbelievably, the same

This Topps prototype card, circa 1970, is labeled "Leroy Kelly" but instead shows a wide out. This card was used only for Topp's design purposes. (Don Butler)

error was repeated in the 1960 set. Wrong Jim Taylor. Yes, the card had him labeled as the Packer fullback, and the card back raved about his accomplishments, but that was the Cardinal line-backer looking on mirthfully. It could be argued, then, that Taylor's rookie card was in 1961, the year Topps finally found a correct photo. It's not technically a variation because corrected cards were not released in 1959 and 1960, but the prices of his rookie and second-year card are significantly lower than if the correct photo was used.

Another potential variation was recently uncovered on Joe Namath's 1965 Topps rookie card. Some versions of the card were found with an odd shaped figure on his left hand, leading some to believe it was a butterfly tattoo. Closer inspection showed it to be just a bit of junk that wound up on the printing plate during that particular run of cards. Since it is not an intentional variation cre-ated by the company, and since the hobby doesn't seem to care one way or the other if it's on the card, no additional value has been placed on the misprinted version (which is just fine to the hobby, since the card can set you back at least $1,300 already). Estimates are one in every ten to fifteen cards contains the "fluff" on Namath's hand.

If you really wanted to get scientific about it, there may be as many as a hundred variations of a single card (not counting such obvious ones as miscuts). Printers realize there is no such thing as a perfect card. Dust always gets on the plates before a card is shot, and printing must occasionally be stopped to wipe off the printing dust. That's why on some cards you sometimes see a black smudge or a pile of glop that doesn't belong; it may be gone on a different card you see. On some of Earl Campbell's 1979 Topps rookie cards, there's a large ink deposit over some of his name. That ink appeared in quite a few cards distributed in the Midwest; unfortunately, it detracts from the value of the card. Something as minor as a dust spot—the type found on that Namath rookie card—would not affect a card's value, but a major misprint such as a double-printed photo (two photos of two different players superimposed on the same card) would drop the value considerably.

Here's a brief list of some of the types of errors and variations you might encounter when you collect football cards.

CROPPING VARIATIONS

A cropping variation is created when a photo is sized or cropped differently on the same card. Since most cropping is very minor, most collectors don't pay much attention to these types of variations.

As an example, in 1990 Score sent three cards to the hobby press announcing its new Series I. One of the cards was Barry Sanders. Months later, when the regular Series I was released, it was discovered the regular issue card and the promotional card—though in every other way alike—were cropped just a little differently. On the regular issue card, the photo is cropped a little tighter on the front (Barry's feet are closer to the border of the bottom of the card) and on the back (the helmet is a little closer to the right border).

As you can tell, it's not very exciting stuff. As a result, only master set collectors care to even try to find these cards. No additional value has been placed on cropping variations.

TEXT VARIATIONS

Text variations occur when a proofreader spots a factual or spelling error on a card that's already been released, goes in the computer, corrects the mistake, and then reissues the card.

Probably the first text variation in football cards came about in the 1954 Bowman set. What probably happened was Baltimore Colt defensive tackle Tom Finnin got a close look at card #97, which spelled his name "Finnan." The thinking is Finnin, who probably signed a contract with Bowman at the time, asked to have a corrected card produced. Bowman did correct it early, and the error card sells today for about $25 while Finnin's corrected card goes for around $3.

Perhaps setting the tone for future sets from other companies, Topps' first professional football player effort in 1956 also contained a text variation. Willard Sherman's card originally appeared without the team name on the front. Topps, of course, could not permit this, and Willard was no doubt relieved to learn he still played for the Rams.

Of course, text errors abound in football—anything from misspellings to statistical errors. As mentioned before, these errors simply remind us that card creators are as prone to mistakes as the rest of us.

One classical example of a blatant text error is in the 1974 Topps set. The back of card #265, Bob Lee, lists him as a member of the Atlanta Hawks instead of the Falcons.

But text errors didn't become real collector concerns until— you guessed it—the 1989 Pro Set. The company's philosophy of correcting any errors that were found mobilized collectors to pay close attention to each card in the hopes of finding an error Pro Set would have to correct. Some of the miscues were fairly insignificant, too—correcting Bobby Hebert's card from "touchdown passers" to "touchdown passes" is getting pretty nitpicky. And Pro Set would no doubt have been forgiven if the company allowed Chuck Noll's card to read "One of three head coaches. . ." instead of correcting it to "One of two head coaches. . ." because of Tom Landry's firing.

SWITCHED NEGATIVE

Another type of error is the switched negative. That means that when the company has the slide separated into colors, it's done so upside down, so the player is looking to the reverse of where he was. With Topps, it happened not once but twice in the 1960 set—with Frank Varrichione and with Hall of Famer Doug Atkins, who's shown wearing not the defensive lineman-ish 81 he was famous for, but the quarterback-ish 18. Chuck Bednarik was probably relieved to know he was still the last two-way player.

A recent example of a switched negative is in the 1990 Action Packed update. The photo on card 56, Eric Green, is reversed on the back of the card. You can clearly see the "Steelers" on his cap is backward.

LETTERING VARIATIONS

These are not to be confused with text variations which are so common in Pro Set. In this type of variation, the actual lettering—usually on the front of the card, such as a player name or team name—is affected. The previously-mentioned 1989 Topps Rodney Holman card is a good example of lettering variations.

A different type of lettering variation occurs in the 1989 Topps set. If you'll look at the card fronts, you'll notice that the first letter in the player's first and last name is red and the rest of the letters are black. It appears that different plates were used to print the names, because in some versions of the cards, the red letters are placed slightly higher than the black letters. Though no official tally has been taken, it appears the off-line variations are scarcer than the regular cards, but plenty can be found.

Lettering variations are very miniscule and aren't very popular collectibles. Since that's the case, very little extra value is put on lettering variations. Like the 1969 off-line lettering variations, none of the 1989 Topps Holman off-line lettering variations carry any extra value.

Holman was victimized by lettering problems in the 1989 Pro Set, too. Unlike the rest of the cards issued that year, "Bengals" was spelled out in capital letters instead of lowercase type. Collectors put up enough of a fuss to have that card corrected in late Series II printings. Since it was corrected so late, it's one of the higher-priced variations in the 1989 Pro Set.

That's not the only 1989 Pro Set lettering variation. The most publicized was Brian Bosworth's card. Like Holman's, Bosworth's team name was printed in capital letters instead of lowercase. It became one of the earliest and easiest variations to find. Though the price was up to $10 in some areas, it's settled to the $2 range for the error version and not much above common price for the corrected version.

SHORT PRINTS

Topps hit a phase in the mid-1960s that bemused and irritated collectors to no end—short prints. Though not technically considered errors or variations, a short-print is a card intended for the regular issue set, but appears in less quantities than the other cards. Short prints come about in two ways: they're either deliberately created that way on the printing sheet or they're hand-pulled after they're printing.

Topps short-printed cards in its football set each year from

This 1963 Fleer Charles Long card was pulled for a checklist. It's one of football's most sought-after short prints. (Don Butler)

1962 through 1965. Because nobody from Topps has volunteered information on why or how some of the cards were printed in lesser quantities than others, we can only make guesses.

Topps has historically printed its cards on 132-card sheets, meaning it randomly places the front and back of each card on an uncut sheet of cardboard. The cardboard is sent through a cutter and the cards are zipped through a collating machine. The cards are arranged on the sheets in eleven rows of twelve cards. That 528 number is important, because if you look back at the last twenty years of Topps cards in any sport, you'll find that most Topps sets consist of 132, 396 or 528 cards—all multiples of 132.

Topps may have played around with 66-sheet formats in the early days, since there were a number of 132- and 198-card sets. Neither card set in 1960 (132 cards) or 1961 (198 cards) are believed to be short-printed, but in 1962, Topps came out with an awkward sized set of 176 cards. A total of 66 cards were short-printed, meaning either one sheet of 66 cards wasn't issued as often or those 66 cards were rotated on 132-card sheets a quarter as often as the other 132 cards. The following year, 76 cards were short-printed in the 170-card set. In 1965, 66 cards were printed in fewer quantities than the rest of the cards.

In the mid-1960s, Topps cards took a decidedly odd turn, as the company experimented again with oversize cards. Topps had tried oversized cards in baseball and had done it in the 1955 All-American football set. In 1965, Topps patterned its football set design and size after the hockey set of the previous fall and went to oversized cards, which created a nightmare for collectors. Because of the odd size of the set, the printing sheets had to be altered. Many were printed twice, compared to once for the rest of the cards. In all, 132 of the 176 cards were short-printed, which works out to three of every four cards. Included in that short-printed batch was the most high-profile football rookie card of modern times—Joe Namath.

This apparently proved to be enough of a disaster to force Topps to abandon the oversize line in football, baseball, and hockey (though it would reppear in three basketball issues in the late 1960s and mid-1970s).

The only other time Topps had experimented with oversized

cards was in the All-American set, which also resulted in short-printed cards. That time, 32 of the 100 cards were short-printed.

Topps was not the only company to have trouble with short-prints. The first Bowman set in 1948, a 108-card effort was printed on three different sheets. Cards 1, 4, 7, 10 and so on were on the first sheet; cards 2, 5, 8, 11 etc., were on the second; and 3, 6, 9, 12 and so on were on the third. No big deal; cards have been printed on separate sheets for years. But for some reason, cards from the first sheet are fairly plentiful while cards from the second sheet are a little tougher, and it's very hard to find the 3/6/9 cards in any condition.

Bowman seemed to iron out its problems, so the next few years' worth of cards were printed in equal quantities. But in 1952, Bowman wanted to try something different. Bowman had seen the success the oversize Topps cards had with collectors, so the company produced two sizes of cards—large and small. The small version was $2^1/16''$ by $3^1/8''$, while the large set was $2^1/2''$ by $3^1/4''$ inches. The sets were exactly the same, except for size. Great idea, bad execution. Because the large-sized cards would not fit onto the regular size Bowman sheet, certain cards could not be included on the initial print run. By looking at a diagram made by football experts Ted Zanidakis and Mike Gallela in the Jan. 3, 1986, issue of *Sports Collectors Digest*, you can see that a Bowman Large sheet contained four rows of eighteen cards, with half the cards being identical. The final eight cards on either end of the sheet—cards 9, 18, 27 and 36, in other words—could not be included in the print run because of the sheet size. Not only that, when they were finally printed, those cards received a lot of damage. Charley Conerly and Joe Stydahar are two of the most valuable of the short-printed cards.

The topper of the 1952 Bowman Large set is the final card, number 144, Jim "Buck" Lansford. It was printed in far fewer quantities than any other card, it received much more damage during printing than any other card, and adding to its current value is the fact it's the last card in the set. Remember, in the old days, collectors kept their sets together through a variety of methods, including rubber bands. The first and last cards in the set usually suffered the most damage, and the same is true with the rare

Lansford card. Very few today can be found in NM condition, and sale prices have ranged from $1,000 to $5,000 and more.

Bowman returned with an oversize issue in 1954, and again gave collectors the joy of short prints. A third of the set—twenty-three of the ninety-six cards—were short-printed, but are considerably easier to find than the 1952 Bowman Large short prints.

Moving ahead eight years—after the 1955 Topps short prints—Frank H. Fleer's company entered its second season of football card production. The 1961 Fleer set included both AFL and NFL players—plus a good dose of short prints. Forty-four of the 220 cards are short-printed, including a Jack Kemp second-year card which can command more than $125 in NM condition (see what the term "presidential potential" can do to your cards?).

Topps, meanwhile, had entered its short-print phase, as discussed above. But Fleer, which entered its fourth and final year of player production (until 1990) in 1963, didn't want to go down without leaving its own mark on the world of short prints. Only two short-printed cards were included in the set, but they're some of the most notorious cards in football history. Not too many football fans remember the names of Charles Long and Bob Dougherty, but they're well-known to football collectors. In 1963, Fleer officials decided to issue a checklist with its set. That was a reasonable thought, except for the fact the cards were already going through the cutter. No problem, Fleer said. We'll just pull a couple of players nobody will miss and put a checklist in their spots on the card sheets. So Long and Dougherty didn't get respect from Fleer back then, but they're getting it from collectors today. A Long card in NM shape can go for $150, while a Dougherty card—which is much tougher to find than the Long card, leading to speculation that the Long card was pulled after the Dougherty card—can go for $250 in the same condition.

COLOR VARIATIONS, MISCUTS, BLANKBACKS, WRONGBACKS

The less popular types of variations have to do with problems that are created while cards are on the printing press.

Cards with color variations simply show a different color on one part of the card than the other regular issues. This can be something as minor as a team name that's pink instead of red (as in the case of four Philadelphia Eagles cards from the 1979 Topps set), or something as major as players with entirely green and blue faces (found in the 1990 Pro Set). In these types of variations, an inkwell of a certain type of color has usually run dry during the coloring process, so the mix of colors is thrown off. While these cards are fun to find, collectors don't put much value on them. They're considered to be basically worthless oddities, unless you find some master set collector who really wants to add unusual items to his collection.

A miscut card is one that has been incorrectly lined up and sent through the cutter. In other words, a whole sheet has been cut wrong, and the top of one player's card might show the bottom of the card above his on the sheet. Miscut cards are considered to be worthless.

Blankbacks or blank fronts have one correctly-printed side of the card, but the other side is completely blank. Again, these are fun to find, but don't command too much money or attention. Blankbacks and wrongbacks have been around since the inception of football cards, but they're not too highly regarded unless they involve some major stars.

A wrongback is simply a card that shows one player on the front, but shows a different player's card back. This occurs when a sheet of different card backs is inserted with the correct card backs before the cards go through a cutter. While they make interesting finds, not too much value is placed on them unless they involve major stars or rookies on the front or back. Then the card can be worth as much as five times its usual value. The 1990 Series I Pro Set proved to be especially bountiful for wrongback collectors. Especially affected were the Pro Bowl cards, which included enough stars to command collector attention to wrongbacks.

Miscuts, blankbacks, wrongbacks and color variations are some of the most common types of errors found today, and most seem to be prevalent in the 1990 Pro Set. That set was Pro Set's first on its new hi-tech printing press; apparently all the bugs weren't worked out.

PHOTO VARIATIONS AND CREATED VARIATIONS

Variations in this category are those that have been intentionally added or subtracted by the card producers. Yes, we know

Another early 1970s Topps
prototype. Note the
basketball used as
background. (Don Butler)

most are already, but this is a catchall category for some of the smaller variations that aren't already defined.

Perhaps a wrong photo has been issued on a player's card and the company doesn't want to look too bad or the NFL asks for a change. Maybe a trademark was missing from the company or team logo, and someone had to stop the presses and paste one on the original. Possibly a player's name was misspelled, or his position was misidentified, or the number of wins was incorrect.

Until the card has actually been corrected and reissued, it's nothing more than an error. For instance, the 1958 Topps rookie card of R.C. Owens shows a white player instead of a black player. This card was not corrected, so it receives no extra value. (The Owens card actually showed Don Owens.) As discussed before, the 1959 and 1960 Topps cards of Jim Taylor show not the Packer HOF running back, but a Cardinal linebacker of the same name.

The photo variations in the 1989 Score issue (see the variation list at the end of the chapter) are excellent examples of photo variations. Photo variations are popular among collectors, but since most companies are outstanding about identifying players nowadays, you don't find too many.

Other created variations include Pro Set's practice of adding "Scouting Photo," "Traded," or "Drafted" stripes to later editions of its cards. These additions may or may not be necessary, but again Pro Set's "living set/fix it" concept has created a new line of variations. Pro Set also has begun to release the most miniscule of variations yet—the addition of the tiny trademark logos to cards on which they were initially omitted or tough to see.

But Pro Set gave the diehard error-finders something to look for. Knowing that Pro Set would correct anything, no matter how insignificant, collectors began poring over each card with a magnifying glass and a football register. Dozens of errors that normally would go unreported suddenly found space in the hobby magazines for Pro Set's 1989 and 1990 issues—for such things as missing trademark and registered logos, stats that read 5 catches for 96 yards instead of 9 catches for 96 yards. The situation reached ridiculous depths in the 1990 Series II, when the majority of the fifteen corrected cards dealt with player positions on the front and back. Backs were changed from G-T to G to correspond with the card front; LB-DE was changed to LB; DE was changed to DT.

Perhaps the silliest of all the Series II corrections was card #785, a photo of Commissioner Paul Tagliabue at the Berlin Wall. The text was changed to read Tagliabue "posed at" the Berlin Wall instead of "peered through" the Berlin Wall.

CARD ODDS AND ENDS

In 1990, Fleer became the fifth company to get an NFL license, joining Topps, Pro Set, Score, and Action Packed. Collectors took to Fleer's first football issue since the early 1960s and made it one of the best sellers of the year. Many, however, took a close look at the card fronts. Hadn't they seen that picture somewhere before?

It turns out they had—like in 1989 and 1990 Score and Pro Set. The exact same photos appeared on either the front or back of cards from two (sometimes three) different companies. How is this possible?

Remember that when most of these companies received their li-

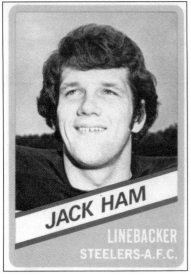 

Duplicated photos: 1976 Wonder Bread (made by Topps) and 1975 Topps regular issue. (Don Butler)

censes, they had little time to assemble a battery of photographers to cover football games. Part of the licensing agreement with the NFL allows card companies to use the NFL's extensive photo library, which contains hundreds of thousands of images (on any given Sunday, a battery of up to eighty NFL-assigned photographers may cover just one game). The card company usually sends its photography department to sort through some of these images for cards. Naturally, they'd pick the best photos—and what one company thinks is the best photo, another company might agree. That's why the same photo of Bo Jackson appeared in the 1989 Pro Set, on the 1989 Score "Great Combos" card, and in the 1990 Fleer issue.

This was hardly new to the card industry. Topps was notorious for using the same football photos year after year. Fred Biletnikoff seemed to have only one photo on file in the Topps library, as it was used twice in the Topps regular series, in a couple of Topps football subsets, and in a couple of food sets Topps was contracted to produce for Bazooka and Kellogg's. The same photos of Jake Scott, Jim Langer, and Bob Griese appeared two or three years in a row—sometimes with the photo a little enlarged, maybe with it shrunk down a little. In the case of HOFer Willie Brown, who appears in the 1975 set and in a food issue released a year earlier, the photo—a head shot—was simply reversed.

It's not clear why Topps used this method, although there are a couple of possible explanations. First, football was nowhere near as popular as baseball so not much money for new photos or effort to get new photos was put into football cards. Topps officials might have reasoned that collectors wouldn't notice the difference. Truthfully, nobody has really picked up on duplicated photos until now. It's also possible Topps couldn't find photographers to send in quality photos year after year. It *is* possible, but maybe Topps simply had an overworked staff which had to get a football, basketball, baseball, and hockey set out, in addition to several non-sport sets, and simply took shortcuts. At any rate, the prospect of finding duplicated photos gives collectors something to search for in old sets.

1989 PRO SET VARIATIONS

Card 47, William Perry. This card was originally issued, but Perry apparently didn't have a contract with the NFL Players Association to release a card. So Perry's card was pulled in favor of Ron Morris. Corrected early; around 10,000 Perry cards were issued. Current value: $40.

Card 53, Mike Ditka. A yellow Hall of Fame stripe was added to his card front midway through the Series II print run. The non-striped card is worth twenty cents: the HOF card goes for seventy-five cents, as fewer were made.

Card 60, Rodney Holman. The uncorrected card reads "BENGALS" on the front, instead of "Bengals" to correspond with the rest of the Pro Set cards. It was finally corrected very late in the Series II/Final Update print run: it's thought that fewer than 10,000 of the corrected "Bengals" version exist. Uncorrected value is twenty cents; the corrected card is worth around $10.

Card 100, John Elway. The uncorrected version reads, "Drafted 1st Round, '83"; corrected version says, "Acquired trade '83." It was one of the first 1989 cards corrected by Pro Set. Uncorrected value is $20, compared to twenty-five cents for the corrected card, which is much easier to find.

Card 193, Stacy Toran. Toran died in a car crash in August 1989, and Pro Set reworked his Series I card in Series II. The updated version has a black stripe in the lower right corner that reads "1961-1989." The text on the back also has been altered and includes the date of Toran's death. The regular issue goes for ten cents; the updated Toran card is valued at seventy-five cents.

Card 214, Ferrell Edmunds. His name was incorrectly spelled "Edmonds" on the front and back of the card. It was corrected to "Edmunds" midway through the Series I print run. The incorrect version is valued at $1.75; the corrected issue—which also appeared in Series II—is worth about twenty cents.

Card 260, Raymond Berry. Like the Mike Ditka card, a yellow Hall of Fame stripe was added to the front of his card. This was added midway through the Series II print run. The regular issue is worth twenty cents; the card with the HOF stripe goes for about seventy-five cents.

Card 266, Bobby Hebert. The original back read, "Threw three touchdown passers in 42-0 rout. . ." This was changed midway through the Series I print run to read "Threw three touchdown passes in 42-0 rout. . ." The error version, being much scarcer, goes for $1.50; his corrected card is worth about a dime.

Card 355, Chuck Noll. The original version, which was written before Tom Landry was axed in Dallas, read, "One of only three current NFL coaches to lead same team for 20 consecutive seasons." It was updated to read, "One of only two current NFL coaches. . ." This was corrected midway through the Series I print run, so his error card goes for seventy-five cents, while the updated card is worth under twenty cents.

Card 363, Anthony Miller. His incorrect touchdown total reads 14.8; it was corrected to 3. This was one of the earliest Pro Set corrections, so the error version is worth about $15 while his corrected card is worth about a quarter.

Card 391, Brian Bosworth. One of the most celebrated variations in Series I, the error version has "Seahawks" in the team affiliation on the front. This didn't fit with the rest of the cards in the set, which listed the city name, so it was corrected to "Seattle". This was corrected midway through the Series I print run. The

"Seahawks" version is worth about seventy-five cents, while the corrected version should go for around a quarter.

Card 404, Curt Warner. The uncorrected back reads, "Seattle's all-time leader in rushing yards (1,455) . . ." It was corrected very early in the Series I print run to say, "Seattle's all-time leader in rushing yards (6,074) . . ." The 1,455 version goes for about $12; the corrected version is about a dime.

Card 478, Jim McMahon. Midway through the Series II print run, a blue traded stripe appeared in the lower right corner of his cards. Non-stripe cards are worth about twenty cents; the updated cards go for about seventy-five cents. In addition, a third version of his card has appeared—the card with the stripe normally has "See Bears card 44" in italic type at the end of the text on the back, but several versions of this card have been found without the note. Since it—and the Byner and Riggs cards also missing the "See" line—seems to be the scarcest of all the 1989 Pro Set variations, each may sell for more than $100.

Card 480, Earnest Byner. Same thing as McMahon's cards—a blue traded stripe appeared midway through the Series II print run. Like McMahon's cards, the "plain" version is worth less than fifteen cents; the striped version can fetch seventy-five cents.

Card 483, Gerald Riggs. Same thing as the McMahon and Byner cards, and corrected at the same time. Non-stripe version goes for less than fifteen cents; the updated card goes for about seventy-five cents.

Card 535, Gizmo Williams. Three versions of his card have turned up. The first one printed, and the first corrected, has NO scouting photo tagline on the front and reads, "Canadian Footbal" in the first line of text on the back. Fewer than 500 are believed to have been made, so the value on the "Canadian Footbal" is more than $100. The second version still doesn't have the scouting photo line on the front, but "Canadian Footbal" was corrected to "Canadian Football" in the text. This version goes for around $1. The corrected version reads "Scouting Photo" in small black type along the side of the card and goes for under a quarter.

Card 539, James Jefferson. The card was originally printed without the blue Pro Set Prospect stripe on the front and

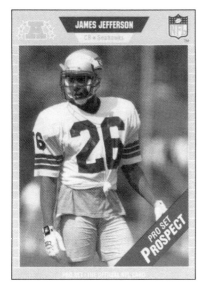

1989 Pro Set's James Jefferson — with and without prospect stripe. (Don Butler)

was corrected fairly early. The non-stripe version fetches about seventy-five cents; the striped version goes for about twenty cents.

1989 SCORE VARIATIONS

Note: all cards were corrected at the same time: very late in the print run. Only late-run wax boxes and very late factory sets contain the corrected cards. Corrected cards may sell for as much as three to five times the price of a regular-issue card.

Card 101, Keith Jackson. Number on back changed from 84 to 88 to match the number shown on his jersey. The uncorrected card goes for around $1.25; the corrected card has sold for $3 to $5.

Card 122, Ricky Sanders. Number on back changed from 46 to 83 to match jersey shown on front. Uncorrected card goes for about fifty cents; corrected card goes for $2 and up.

Card 126, Ron Hall. Photos were corrected on front and back. Original photos showed a black player; Hall is white.

Uncorrected cards sell for around fifty cents; corrected cards go for $2 or so.

Card 188, Mark Carrier. Original photo on the back showed a helmetless player with a "Fu Manchu" and a headband. Corrected photo shows Carrier wearing a helmet and no gaudy mustache. Uncorrected card sells for $1; corrected goes for $2 to $3.

Card 218, Willie Gault. Original front showed #93, Greg Townsend, rumbling downfield with the football (the "9" is slightly scrunched up). The corrected front shows a similar pose, but Gault is clearly wearing an 83. Uncorrected card goes for a buck; corrected card goes for $2 to $3.

Card 293, Keith Jackson All-Pro. As on his regular card, the original card listed his jersey as 84. It was corrected to 88. Uncorrected goes for $1; corrected goes for $2 to $3.

Card 305, Tim Brown. The original card showed #80, James Lofton, in a white jersey. The corrected card showed Brown, #81, in a black jersey. Uncorrected card goes for around $1; corrected card can fetch $2 to $3.

Card 316, Eric Thomas. Error back listed his jersey as 34 and his position as RB; the card was corrected to 22 and CB. Error version goes for around seventy-five cents; corrected card is worth around $1.50.

1990 PRO SET VARIATIONS

Card 2, Joe Montana. In later editions, Jim Kelly's stats in the text were corrected from 3,521 yards to 3,130 yards. Since it was corrected late in the print run, the corrected version is valued at $1 to $2. The uncorrected card is worth thirty to fifty cents.

Card 15, Walter Stanley. Back listed his number either as 8 or 86, with the 8 version being much tougher to find. That version goes for $7 to $10, while the corrected card is a common.

Card 18, Chris Doleman. In later editions, Lawrence Taylor's sack total was changed from 104 to 104.5; Greg Townsend's name, previously spelled "Townsent," was corrected; and Jim Jeffcoat's name was corrected from "Jeffcoact." Since it was corrected late in the print run, the corrected version goes for $1 to $2; the incorrect card is common.

Card 19, Andre Ware. Later editions have a red drafted stripe. Also, the back was changed to read WR-KR and was changed from "1990 Downtown Athletic Club, New York" to "Registered Service Mark of the Downtown Athletic Club, NYC." The non-stripe card goes for fifty cents; the striped version can fetch $1.

Card 20, Mohammed Elewonibi. Later editions have a red drafted stripe. The non-stripe version is fifteen to twenty-five cents; the updated card goes for seventy-five cents.

Card 21, Percy Snow. Later editions have a red drafted stripe. The original card is worth twenty cents; the updated card with the stripe is valued at seventy-five cents.

Card 22, Anthony Thompson. Later editions have a red drafted stripe. The non-stripe card is valued at fifty cents; the corrected card goes for $1.25.

Card 25, Franco Harris. In later editions, the birthdate was corrected from 2/7/50 to 3/7/50. The incorrect version is valued at a dime, and the corrected card is worth about fifty cents.

Card 27, Jack Lambert. In later editions, the birthdate was corrected from 7/2/52 to 7/8/52. The incorrect version is valued at a dime, and the corrected card is worth about fifty cents.

Card 63, Ricky Dixon. Stats are missing under his bio notes in the uncorrected version. Error cards are tough to find and are valued at between $7 to $9.

Card 68, Sam Wyche. As with Dixon, statistical data was added to later editions. Error cards are also tough to find and are likewise valued at $7 to $9.

Card 75, Ozzie Newsome. Birthplace was corrected from Little Rock, AR, to Muscle Shoals, AL. Corrected versions are much tougher to find. The uncorrected card is worth a dime; the corrected card is worth about $2.

Card 110, Johnny Holland. Error version shows no name and position at the top of the card. Corrected relatively early, though error cards showed up in late-run wax boxes. Like the Dixon and Wyche cards, the incomplete versions usually sell for between $7 to $9.

Card 111, Perry Kemp. Error back showed teammate Ken Stills in a gray t-shirt; this was changed to show Kemp in a green shirt. Corrected very early, though some error versions showed up in late-run wax boxes. The Ken Stills card sell for between $7 to $10.

Card 114, Sterling Sharpe. Birthplace on back was changed from Glenville, GA, to Chicago, IL. The uncorrected card is worth thirty-five cents; the corrected version goes for $3 to $5.

Card 152, Mervyn Fernandez. In later editions, bio notes were corrected from "Free agent '87" to "Drafted 10th round '83." Corrected midway through the print run. The original version sells for fifteen cents; the corrected card goes for fifty cents to $1.

Card 161, Art Shell. In later editions, birthdate was corrected from 11/25/46 to 11/26/46. Very difficult to find; only appeared in late-run wax boxes. The updated version can be found for $3 to $5.

Card 210 Morten Andersen, 216 Eric Martin, and 221 Jim Mora. In early boxes, card numbers and player names were printed in white on the back; they were changed to black to correspond with the rest of the Saints team. Either version is pretty easy to find, and shouldn't cost you more than a quarter to fifty cents.

Card 289, Charles Haley. In later editions, stats were corrected from 1 fumble recovery in 1986 and 4 total to 2 in 1986 and 5 total. Probably the toughest Series I variation to find. The corrected version, if you can find it, usually sells for about $7 to $10.

Card 319, Ray Perkins. Like the Johnny Holland card, the early version is missing his name and title at the top of the back. Also like the Holland card, some of these showed up in late run wax boxes. Incomplete cards are valued at $7 to $9.

Card 343, Chris Hinton. The corrected version has a traded stripe. This was one of the first Pro Set 1990 corrections and is getting hard to find. Non-striped versions can fetch anywhere from $2 to $10.

Super Bowl insert 22. A wrong date on the reverse originally read January 31, 1989. It was corrected to 1988. Corrected fairly early in the print run, so the error card is worth $3 to $5.

SERIES II

Note: the corrected versions of these cards were released almost all at once. The original error versions are generally valued at a nickel or a dime more than the corrected cards.

Card 449, Dan Hampton. Uncorrected back reads DE; corrected back reads DT to correspond with card front. Uncorrected card is valued slightly higher than the easier-to-find corrected card.

Card 496, Kevin Glover. Back changed from C-G to C to correspond with card front. Like the Hampton card, the error version was corrected early.

Card 607, Wes Hopkins. The fumble/interception headings were changed in color from black over red to red. The corrected version is the most common.

Card 626, Rod Woodson. The fumble/interception headings were changed in color from black over red to red. The corrected version is the most common.

Card 627, Rod Bernstine. Back was changed from TE to RB to correspond with the card front.

Card 630, Anthony Miller. Back was changed from WR to WR-KR.

Card 632, Leslie O'Neal. Front was changed from LB-DE to LB to correspond with the card back.

Card 633, David Richards. Back was changed from G-T to G to correspond with the card back.

Card 657, Curt Jarvis. "The Official NFL Card" was added to the top of the front. It's missing in early versions.

Card 698, Terry Wooden. The number on the back was changed from 51 to 90 to correspond with the card front.

Card 723, Oliver Barnett. The front was changed from DT to NT. This is believed to be the earliest Series II correction, as both error and corrected versions were found in very early boxes.

Card 743, Johnny Bailey. The number on the back was changed from 46 to 22 to correspond with the card front.

Card 744, Eric Moore. A "Pro Set Prospect" stripe, missing from early versions, was added.

Card 785, Berlin Wall newsreel. The text on the back was changed from "peered through the Berlin Wall" to "posed at the Berlin Wall."

1990 FLEER VARIATIONS

Card 10, Joe Montana. Uncorrected version has touchdown and yard headings reversed on the back. The uncorrected version, pulled early, sells for $10 to $15.

Card 83, Byron Evans. Originally numbered as 82, the error card goes for about $1.

Card 84, Ron Heller. Originally numbered as 83, the error card goes for about $1.

Card 158, Jim Lachey. Later versions of this card have a thin rule added beneath the bio notes. No additional value has been added.

Card 162, Mark May. Later versions of the card have a thin black rule added beneath the bio notes. No additional value has been added.

Card 289, Kevin Butler. Four variations exists: one reads Punter on the front with a "P" or "PK" on the back; the other reads Placekicker on the front with either a "P" or a "PK" on the back. Correct version is Punter/P. Each incorrect version goes for about $15.

Card 290, Jim Covert. Later versions of the card have a thin black rule added beneath the bio notes. No additional value has been added.

1990 SCORE VARIATIONS

Card 134, Kevin Butler. Scarcer photo on back shows him wearing a helmet; corrected photo shows him without a helmet. "Error" card is about a dime more than the "corrected" card.

Card 136, Vai Sikahema. Scarcer photo on back shows him wearing a helmet; corrected photo shows him without a helmet. "Error" card is about a dime more than the "corrected" card.

Card 147, Joey Browner. Both versions on back show him without a helmet. Uncorrected one has him looking up into the sun—you can see most of his face. The new version has him looking off to the left; you can see only one side of his face. No additional value has been added.

Card 208, Ralf Mojsiejenko. Original stats on the back listed him with the Chargers. It was corrected to read Redskins. Error version is worth about $1 to $2 more than the corrected version.

Card 600, Buck Buchanan. Uncorrected back says he was the first player selected in the 1983 AFL draft; it was corrected to read the '63 draft. Corrected version is worth about a dime more.

The Hall of Fame

As alluded to in previous chapters, selection to the Pro Football Hall of Fame has an important impact on the price of a player's card. As a recent example, offensive lineman Bob St. Clair, who opened holes for Hugh McElhenny and Joe Perry from the 49ers' "Million Dollar Backfield," was selected by the veterans' committee in 1990. Prior to that, his cards had all been commons; his rookie card from the 1955 Bowman set, which you could have picked up in 1989 for a few bucks, is now worth more than $20, with his subsequent cards several dollars over the common mark.

Football card collectors take great interest in the Hall of Fame. It's quite a bit different than baseball, where you have a pretty good idea of who will be inducted during the latter stages of his career and in the years before the actual announcement. In football, especially for the non-yard-producing positions (which is most of them), it's a difficult call as to who gets in. Sure, you can be fairly certain a perennial All-Pro such as Anthony Munoz, Lawrence Taylor, or Ronnie Lott should get in on the first try, but what about a guy like Too Tall Jones? Bob

Griese, who led Miami to three straight Super Bowl appearances and the NFL's only perfect season, was passed over by the Hall of Fame five times until his 1990 selection by the old-timers committee. Lynn Swann and L.C. Greenwood, two of the most prominent names from the Steelers' glory years, have yet to get in. Why?

As mentioned before, much of the selection process is a judgement call. Was the player dominant during his day? And did he have an impact on the game? As in the cases above, the answers might be yes and yes, but that still won't get you a bronze bust and a wild August weekend in Canton.

The Hall of Fame's selection process, as mentioned earlier, is one of the most rigorous of all the professional sports halls of fame. The only drawback is four to seven new members are *required* to be elected each year. The election of new members falls entirely upon a thirty-member Board of Selectors, which is made up mainly of sportswriters (one from each NFL city, with two from New York; another represents the Pro Football Writers Association; the final is an at-large board member).

This group meets the day before the Super Bowl each year to pick that year's class of enshrinees. Fans can help in the process by nominating any contributor or player (players must have been retired at least five years; a coach just needs to be retired)—all you have to do is write the Pro Football Hall of Fame.

From the list of nominees, the Board of Selectors votes on who should be in the Hall. A candidate needs about 82 percent of the vote to be enshrined. The winners are announced the day before the Super Bowl and are formally enshrined in Canton during the first weekend in August.

As mentioned before, current rules call for four to seven new enshrinees per year. Does that mean some unworthy players are in the Hall of Fame? Not at all. In fact, several deserving players have so far been overlooked. Unlike baseball, where the Veterans Committee has made some terrible choices for the Hall of Fame, the Pro Football Hall of Fame's Board of Selectors is to be congratulated for being conservative in their approach. But being forced to pick four to seven new members a year may mean quite a bit of overcrowding in the next twenty-five years.

PICKING FUTURE HOFers

With so many specialized players these days, there are a number of factors which the HOF voters seem to require for admission. Two in particular stand out: number of All-Pro years and participation in championships.

Being named All-Pro or selected to the Pro Bowl is especially important for offensive linemen and defensive players, since there are few comparative statistics that would separate one player from another. Being recognized as a Pro Bowler means the players you battle week in and week out think you're one of the best in the game. If you're good enough to make the Pro Bowl as selected by the NFL players, that should be enough evidence for the HOF committee, which obviously can't watch every player every game.

Another big determining factor is the number of championships or number of times a team has played in an important game. Vince Lombardi's Packers and Chuck Noll's Steelers were two of the all-time greatest teams, and each has—or will have—more than ten members inducted into the Hall of Fame. The Packers have Bart Starr, Jim Taylor, Paul Hornung, Forrest Gregg, Jim Ringo, Ray Nitschke, Willie Wood, Vince Lombardi, Herb Adderley, Willie Davis, and Em Tunnell, with Henry Jordan and Jerry Kramer strong possibilities on the veterans ballot. The Steelers have Jack Lambert, Franco Harris, Jack Ham, Terry Bradshaw, Mel Blount, Joe Greene, and Art Rooney and will get at least three more including Chuck Noll, Mike Webster, Lynn Swann, and possibly John Stallworth and Donnie Shell.

Here's a breakdown of some other dynasties:

The 1950s Lions with Jack Christiansen, Yale Lary, Bobby Layne, Dick Lane, and Joe Schmidt.

The 1950s Browns with Otto Graham, Marion Motley, Paul Brown, Dante Lavelli, and Lou Groza (Jim Brown was part of the 1960s dynasty).

The 1950s-1960s Colts with John Unitas, Ray Berry, Lenny Moore, Bobby Mitchell, Jim Parker, Weeb Ewbank, Gino Marchetti, and Art Donovan.

The 1960s Bears with Mike Ditka, Doug Atkins, Stan Jones, Bill George, Dick Butkus, George Halas, and Gale Sayers.

The 1950s Rams with Bob Waterfield, Tom Fears, Norm Van Brocklin, and Elroy Hirsch; a decade later, the dynasty turned over to include Merlin Olsen and Deacon Jones.

The 1950s-1960s Giants had Frank Gifford, Sam Huff, Y.A. Tittle, and Andy Robustelli.

The 1970s Raiders featured Fred Biletnikoff, Ted Hendricks, George Blanda, Jim Otto, Art Shell, and Gene Upshaw.

The 1970s Cowboys had Tom Landry, Roger Staubach, Bob Lilly, and certain future inductees Tony Dorsett and Randy White.

The 1960s Chiefs had Buck Buchanan, Bobby Bell, Willie Lanier, and Len Dawson.

The 1930s Packers had Mike Michalske, Curley Lambeau, Don Hutson, Arnie Herber, Clarke Hinkle, and Johnny "Blood" McNally.

The 1950s-1960s 49ers had Bob St. Clair, Hugh McElhenny, Joe Perry, Ollie Matson, and Y.A. Tittle.

In current times, only two truly memorable dynasties have fewer than five HOFers—the current San Francisco 49ers (with

1986 Topps Jerry Rice rookie. A sure HOFer with a card that should rise in value. (Don Butler)

1984 Topps Roger Craig
rookie, an
underappreciated card.
(Don Butler)

only three sure shots—Joe Montana, Jerry Rice, and Bill Walsh,
with Roger Craig a strong candidate) and the 1970s Dolphins, who
boast only Bob Griese, Larry Csonka, Paul Warfield, and Jim
Langer in the Hall of Fame. Don Shula is a lock when he decides
to retire. So it's not a given that when a team dominates for a number of years that most of the offense and/or defense will automatically be inducted into the Hall. In the case of the 49ers and the
Dolphins, HOF voters felt the teams' system was as responsible for
the titles as the players.

     When you break down the Hall of Fame by position, you'll
notice immediately that the glamor players—quarterbacks, wide
receivers, running backs—are the top three most populated areas.
Twenty-one quarterbacks are enshrined, followed by eighteen
wideouts and eighteen halfbacks. Linebackers occupy the fourth
spot with twelve, followed by executive/owners with eleven. Six
coaches and six fullbacks are tied in the fifth spot. Defensive tackle
was next with eight, followed by defensive end with seven and offensive guards with seven. Six centers and six safeties are in the
Hall of Fame, and the lone tight end to be inducted so far is Mike

Ditka (although John Mackey should get in someday, as will Ozzie Newsome).

Keeping in mind those two key factors, Pro Bowl and championships, let's take a look at some of the current and recently retired players who may or may not have a shot at the Hall of Fame.

Of the recently retired players, several are sure shots. Walter Payton, of course, is a lock, as is Steve Largent. The certain HOF election of both boosted their card prices to the $300 and $100 range, respectively.

But two other certain HOFers—running backs, no less—haven't received as much attention. John Riggins is one of only a handful of players to rush for more than 10,000 yards. He was the key man in the Redskin offense that won a Super Bowl. But his 1972 rookie card can still be found for under $10. When he's elected to the Hall, expect that price to at least double, since the 1972 set is a collector favorite to piece together anyway.

The other undervalued sure-shot HOFer is Tony Dorsett, whose 1978 Topps rookie card still sells for about $40 or so. Mysteriously, his card didn't start rising in value until halfway through the second year of the late 1980s football boom.

Other sure HOFers (in our opinion) and their rookie card prices include:

Dan Fouts (1975 Topps—$40).

Charlie Joiner (1972 Topps—$12.50, what a bargain!). Joiner was one of Fout's favorite receivers.

Randy White (1976 Topps—$12.50).

Mike Haynes (1977 Topps—$2.50). This has to be one of the best bargains out there. Haynes owns a Super Bowl ring from his Raider days and went to the Pro Bowl *nine* times.

Harold Carmichael (1974 Topps—$7.50). *Sports Collectors Digest* writer Tol Broome compared his career with that of current HOFer Fred Biletnikoff. Carmichael leads in receptions 590 to 589, in yards 8,974 to 8,974, and in touchdowns 79 to 76. Carmichael played in plenty of Pro Bowls and went to a Super Bowl with the Eagles in 1980.

Ray Guy (1974 Topps—$4). He should be the second true specialist right behind 1991 inductee Jan Stenerud.

As mentioned before, the HOF committee is required to se-

Dan Fouts' 1975 Topps
rookie card. $40 to $50 for
this HOFer. (Don Butler)

lect at least one old-timer a year to the Hall of Fame. Here are a
few we feel have been overlooked.

Larry Little (1972 Topps—$1). Little paved the path for
Csonka, Jim Kiick, and Mercury Morris to batter opponents with a
running game; he also protected Bob Griese and Earl Morrall
when they had to pass. Little should join center Jim Langer in the
Hall of Fame. He was a six-time All-Pro in fourteen years.

John Mackey (1964 Philadelphia—$7.50). In 1989,
former superstar running back Jim Brown made a stink because
Mackey was not elected to the Hall of Fame. Mike Ditka also be-
lieves Mackey was one of the greatest tight ends ever. Since there
is a grand total of one tight end currently in the Hall of Fame and
his name is Mike Ditka, he isn't a bad judge of talent. Mackey was
All-Pro plenty of times with the Colts and will eventually make the
Hall of Fame, probably in a year when the competition isn't as stiff
as it has been recently.

John Stallworth (1978 Topps—$2). It's a tossup between
Stallworth and teammate Lynn Swann, and both could make the

Hall. Stallworth could be the first one in, though, as his career lasted longer (fourteen seasons to nine), impressive numbers in the Steelers' four Super Bowl wins (11 catches, 268 yards, three touchdowns) and his No. 23 ranking on the career receptions list should outweigh his lone Pro Bowl appearance when the voters make their choices.

Mike Webster (1977 Topps—$2). He's a sure bet to make the Hall. An eight-time Pro Bowler and owner of four Super Bowl rings, he plowed the way for Franco Harris and protected Terry Bradshaw.

Ken Anderson (1973 Topps—$12.50). Anderson quietly put together an outstanding career. He ranks sixth on the all-time completion percentage list and ranks fourth in completions; Anderson also ranks seventh in career passing yardage and fifteenth in career touchdown passes. He took the Bengals to the Super Bowl in 1981, which should help his cause.

Mick Tingelhoff (1964 Philadelphia—$3). Who? you ask. Mick manned the center of the Minnesota offensive line for seventeen seasons during the 1960s and 1970s. He established a record for centers by being named All-Pro for seven straight seasons (1964 to 1970). He's been eligible for election for nearly a decade; obviously hurting his election are all those Super Bowl losses. Mick will eventually make it.

John Brodie (1961 Topps—$30). Under Brodie, the 49ers made it to the NFC Championship game in 1970 and 1971, but lost twice to Dallas. That has hurt his chances (he's been eligible for HOF election for well over a decade). But when you break it down, you find Brodie ranks in the top ten in all-time attempts (seventh), completions (sixth), yards (ninth), and touchdowns (ninth). Brodie was a classy man on and off the field.

Paul Krause (1965 Philadelphia—$2). The former Redskin and Viking lasted sixteen NFL seasons and established the record for interceptions with eighty-one. There are three factors the HOF voters obviously see working against Krause—first, he gathered many of his interceptions by being Minnesota's designated "center-fielder"; second, he "only" had three All-Pro nominations; and third, it's that Viking curse that afflicts other stellar players such as Ed White, Carl Eller and Ron Yary.

Jack Youngblood (1973 Topps—$6.50). This five-time All-Pro defensive end manned one of the best defenses of the 1970s. The Rams always were knocked out of the playoffs, though. Still, he should make the Hall in a few years.

Jerry Kramer (1959 Topps—$6). He was picked to the NFL's 50th anniversary all-time team at guard and was also named to the 25th Super Bowl Anniversary team as one of two starting guards. So why isn't this Green Bay Packer great in the Hall? He was All-Pro numerous times, and the way he came back from numerous injuries to regain superior form is exactly the type of profile the Hall of Fame likes.

Now let's take a look at current players and their chances for the Hall.

The certain Hall of Famers include:

Eric Dickerson (1984 Topps—$25).

Howie Long (1984 Topps—$1). He's only thirty-one and has six Pro Bowl appearances.

Ronnie Lott (1982 Topps—$17.50). Lott has eight Pro Bowl seasons in nine years.

Dan Marino (1984 Topps—$30).

Art Monk (1981 Topps—$30). Monk should break Steve Largent's all-time reception mark in 1992.

Joe Montana (1981 Topps—$250).

Anthony Munoz (1982 Topps—$3). He's been labeled as one of the greatest offensive linemen ever and has never missed a game. Munoz and John Hannah have been the two most dominating linemen of the 1970s and 1980s.

Ozzie Newsome (1979 Topps—$7.50). Known as a tremendous blocker, Cleveland also used his pass-catching ability to make the playoffs plenty of times in the 1980s. Though he has participated in only three Pro Bowls, he ran an astonishing fifth on the all-time receptions list.

Jerry Rice (1986 Topps—$50).

Mike Singletary (1983 Topps—$5). The heart and soul of the Bears defense has been to seven Pro Bowls.

Lawrence Taylor (1982 Topps—$22.50).

As for players who may have a shot at the Hall of Fame with a few outstanding seasons or a key playoff win, they include Marcus

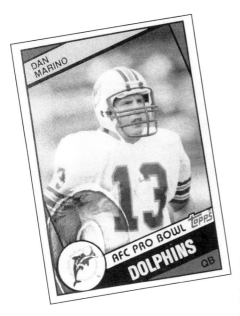

Dan Marino's 1984 Topps rookie card rose from $15 in June 1990 to $35 in January 1991 as spectators fueled interests in his HOF chances. (Don Butler)

Allen (five Pro Bowls), Joey Browner (five), Michael Carter (three), Deron Cherry (six), Mark Clayton (four), Roger Craig (four), Chris Doleman (three), Ray Donaldson (four), Dave Duerson (four), Mark Duper (three), John Elway (three), Bob Golic (three), Darrell Green (three), Russ Grimm (four), Jay Hilgenberg (five), Chris Hinton (six), Ricky Jackson (four), Joe Jacoby (four), Steve Jordan (four), Too Tall Jones (yes, we know he's no longer active, but he has a pretty good shot with three Pro Bowls behind him), Mike Kenn (five), Albert Lewis (three), James Lofton (seven), Charles Mann (three), Clay Mathews (four), Karl Mecklenburg (five), Mike Merriweather (three), Keith Millard (two), Frank Minnifield (four), Max Montoya (three), Warren Moon (two), Stanley Morgan (four), Mike Munchak (five), Jackie Slater (six), Fred Smerlas (three), Bruce Smith (three), Doug Smith (three), Dennis Smith (three), Andre Tippett (five), Al Toon (three), Reggie White (four), Fredd Young (four), and Gary Zimmerman (three).

Of that bunch, the ones we feel have the best chance at HOF entrance—considering their age, their status, and the number of

Joe Montana's rookie card has risen from $20 in 1989 to $250 in 1990. (Don Butler)

Pro Bowls they've seen are Allen, Cherry, Elway, Hinton, Too Tall Jones, Lofton, Mecklenburg, Bruce Smith, and Reggie White.

Then there are the younger stars who aren't in position yet to be considered for the Hall of Fame. The best of the younger players who, with five or six more Pro Bowl-type seasons, would be good bets for the Hall include Barry Sanders, Sterling Sharpe, Don Majkowski, Jim Lachey, Andre Reed, Kent Hull, Bobby Humphrey, Erik McMillan, and Jerry Gray.

What does that tell you? As discussed in chapter 6, pay attention to the position of the player. Collectors will find the current high-profile offensive players (Barry Sanders, Don Majkowski, Sterling Sharpe, Jerry Rice, Joe Montana, Dan Marino) to be relatively expensive right now, but that's because many feel they're stars on the way up or are already headed for the Hall of Fame. Collectors with less money to spend should take a closer look at linebackers and linemen; these cards will take much longer to appreciate (or depreciate) in value, but if you're buying surefire HOFers such as Anthony Munoz, Ronnie Lott, and Mike Singletary, you won't lose.

Again, it's wise to pay attention to the number of times a player makes it to the Pro Bowl during his career. If he gets there more than, say, four times and is still fairly young (under twenty-nine or so), it's a good idea to start searching for his rookie or second-year card. The way his team finishes year in and year out is also a major factor in his HOF potential. If you look through the HOF roster, there are isolated cases of a great player from a mediocre team making the grade, but more often than not the great players have been on winning teams.

The best way to keep track of all this information, of course, is to read the card backs. All the info you need is there. When you read Jay Hilgenberg's card back, you'll find out he's been to five or six straight Pro Bowls, he's only thirty-one years old, he's played on numerous conference winners, and he's played in a Super Bowl. That's starting to sound like a Hall of Fame career.

Not Just Cards

Although cards are the most widely collected of all the sports memoribilia available, there are a number of other items that are highly collectible.

Collecting something different can be fun; sure there are millions collecting football cards today, but how many are collecting autographs of every NFL player to wear jersey Number 1 in the history of the NFL? How about collecting patches from each of the twenty-five Super Bowls?

The list of football-related collectibles is countless. As you venture into an area just remember some of the basic rules. Rule number one is have fun. That's what all collecting is about. Rule number two is try to concentrate your collecting to a specific area or a specific number of items. Rule number three, look everywhere to find this kind of stuff. Finally, rule number four, don't forget rule number one.

AUTOGRAPHS

This is one of the area already jammed with collectors. There is something special about having an autograph. It also becomes

A 1935 Rose Bowl
program and ticket stub. In
1935 it was Alabama and
Stanford. (Chuck Bennett)

more meaningful for you to get the autograph yourself. When you
go the games in your area, bring along cards of your favorite players and those of the opposing team. Make sure you have an autograph pen (Sharpies are the best) and hang around the area where
the teams come out. Always be polite to the players, because there
are hundreds of people who would love to have their autograph.

As for some of the retired stars, check to see if any autograph
guest will be at local shows. Football stars have become great autograph guests the past couple of years and you'll get a chance to
meet some of the greats from years past.

Sometimes if you are lucky, you might get an address of one
of your favorite stars. If you send a letter to their home address, be
sure to send a self-addressed stamped envelope (SASE) to pay for
the return of your valuables. Also, don't send expensive cards
through the mail. Players often get thousands of letters at home
and through the public relations office of their team. Send one of
their newer cards and only ask for one or two autographs.

A 1941 Orange Bowl
program. In 1941 it was
Mississippi State vs.
Georgetown. (Chuck
Bennett)

The *first* Fiesta Bowl
program in 1971 featured
Florida State University and
Arizona State University.
(Chuck Bennett)

A 1936 Sugar Bowl
program. Note that in 1936
the program sold for .25.

Autographs of deceased players have increased value and autographs of Hall of Fame players can reach the $100 mark. Who is next to join the Hall of Fame?

Just about anything is good for an autograph: cards, magazines, game programs etc. Take your pick and experiment. I have seen some pretty nice autographed magazine covers that were framed and matted.

GAME PROGRAMS

Under each category you can find subcategories to help you along your way. You might want to collect game programs for every game you attend. You might try collecting every game program for your favorite team.

Collecting game programs can be fun and very informative. Reading through older game programs you can learn much about the top teams and stars of that era.

There are also some special game programs. When Steve Largent retired from the Seattle Seahawks, not a game program

A 1927 Army vs. Navy
program. (Chuck Bennett)

could be found after the game. The Seattle public relations department did a great job in making that program a collectible item. The
best place to find programs is in the cities of the NFL teams. Also
keep your eye out for game programs of the different leagues like
USFL, WLAF, WFL, and the old AFL.

MEDIA GUIDES

Each NFL team produces a media guide every year. Media
guides are loaded with information and photos of your favorite
players. Records, franchise information, and history are also included in most every media guide.

You can write to the teams for information about purchasing
the new media guides. Each NFL team address is in appendix A in
the back of this book.

As for older media guides, you have to beat the bushes to
come up with some of them. If you have a relative working at a
newspaper or magazine, check with them.

Rose Bowl Tickets: 1932, 1939, 1951, 1956. (Chuck Bennett)

TICKETS

In recent years, tickets have become hot collectibles. Most collectors want full stubbed unused game tickets, but many of the tickets were torn and they are hard to find intact.

Game tickets of games with special meaning tend to bring more money and are more collectible. As with cards, there is a supply and demand to everything collectible. If you want game tickets for Walter Payton's last home game in Chicago, you'll need to spend more than if you were looking just for a Bears' game ticket.

Check the classified ads in the back of some of the hobby magazines. There you'll find collectors trying to fill in their collections by trading their doubles.

PHOTOGRAPHS

Teams have always given away team photographs and photos of their top players. These too have become collectible and the black & white 8 × 10 are great for autographs.

Besides the free photos team provide, there are Associated Press wire photos, postcards and just plain old photos. Collectors have gone to great lengths to frame and matte older photos.

Some of these current photos can be found by writing the teams, and for the older photos and postcards, you'll need to look around.

GAME EQUIPMENT

Just about everything a player wears can be considered collectible. There are people who collect game-worn jerseys, helmets, shoes, wrist bands, pants, etc.

Game-worn jerseys (and equipment) of some of the top players in the league may be costly. Seattle Seahawk equipment manager Walt Loeffler says jerseys of the retired Steve Largent run between $1,000 and $1,500.

During Largent's last season, Loeffler did something special. After each game Loeffler took the jersey that Largent wore and sewed in the date of the game so that there would be sixteen game-worn jerseys.

Helmets can also become costly. Also when you pick up a game helmet, they are no longer to be used; rather they are a piece of history.

Jerseys are popular football collectibles. (Don Butler)

PRESS PINS

All types of pins are collectible, but each year at the Super Bowl, press pins are given to the media covering the game. There have been twenty-five Super Bowls and the farther you go back, the more expensive they get.

AWARDS

These items are, in general, harder to find and more costly, but there are a number of items available to the collector. There are awards, like rings, watches, trophies, etc., given annually to players, administration and team personnel.

Look in the hobby publications and check some of the auctions. Awards and personal items from Hall of Fame players, retired players, and deceased players usually bring high price tags.

SUPER BOWL COLLECTIBLES

You can throw just about anything involved with the Super Bowl into this category. There are game programs, patches, media pins and media gifts.

The past two Super Bowl Card Shows have been great places to find some older Super Bowl memoribilia.

Just remember keep looking to discover some of the wonderful things that can become collectible. Flea markets are great places to find unwanted sports memoriablia. Check in grandmother's basement or with your aunts and uncles. Occasionally you can find items at antique shows and stores. Check your Sunday paper for people having garage sales. Call them and ask to see if they have any football cards or related items.

Pricing Your Cards

You just opened a pack of 1991 Pro Set, and lo and behold, there's a third-year Barry Sanders card. What is it worth? There are a number of price guides available to give you that answer.

But how is that price determined? There are two factors that—like any other commodity—truly determine how much your card is worth. They are scarcity and demand.

These days it's foolish to call any mass produced card scarce. Though card companies do not give out any information on the amount of cards they print, it's estimated that each company prints several hundreds of thousands to even millions for each sport each year. Pro Set, which has far and away the largest print run of any football card company, is usually valued the lowest because Pro Set cards (except, of course, for the promo cards and scarce variations) are available in more places than any other football card. No scarcity, no demand.

Pro Set solves this problem by admitting it will correct any error it finds. The demand for these variations, which can be corrected either early or late in the print run, sends collectors scrambling to buy more Pro Set to add a highly-valued card to their collections. Pro Set thus is able to sell more cards than if it did not correct its errors. As an example, in the 1990 Pro Set Series I, Charles Haley's card #249 sported a minor change—his statistics were corrected from one fumble recovery in 1986 and a total of four to two in 1986 and a total of five. This was one of the hardest of the Series I variations to find—values ranged from $5 to $15—and because of its scarcity, those interested in the Pro Set variations continued to buy the late run wax packs long after they normally would have. Pro Set was able to sell through a lot more cards than it would have if a late-run card was not corrected. Nobody admits to playing the card game this way, since it will look like it's taking advantage of the card buyer, but this is how it works.

Purists may not like it, but the current buyers of today's cards finds value in scarcer variations. Pro Set is in business to sell cards and make money.

Card prices, as in all other commodities prices, are determined by supply and demand. Just because you have the card of a popular rookie doesn't mean it will automatically escalate in value. An excellent example is the 1989 Barry Sanders Pro Set card. Even if the factors are right for the card—Sanders makes the Hall of Fame, Pro Set continues to issue cards, the set is popular—the card will still hold no more than a third of the value of the 1989 Score Barry Sanders card. Score printed its football run in far less quantity than Pro Set. Now collectors/speculators have forced the price of the Score card to near-investor levels, while the Pro Set card still remains at the "collectible" level. Scarcity should always be a prime consideration if you're in it for the money.

The flip side to the scarcity rule is the demand rule. Though Pro Set had probably double the print run as Topps in 1989, the prices for rookie cards such as Don Majkowski and Ickey Woods are the same or higher in Pro Set. If you abide simply by supply and demand, Topps prices should be about 50 percent higher. But today's collectors like Pro Set a lot more than they like Topps, so there's much more interest and movement in the Pro Set rookies than in the Topps rookies. So even if a nationally issued set is scarce compared to another set from the same year, the lack of demand for the smaller set will keep the prices low.

Demand and scarcity have a symbiotic relationship in cards. If collectors want more Topps cards, you can bet Topps will have more cards the following year. This was the case in 1984, when Topps saturated the market with football cards; that's why prices on the Marino, Dickerson and Elway cards are relatively low compared to other cards from the late 1970s—early 1980s.

On the other hand, if a company produces a scarce product that collectors like, the demand goes through the roof and drives values to incredible heights. The 1989 Score football cards are examples of that. Since it was the first year in football cards for Score, the company wanted to be reasonably sure it would produce enough cards to meet the demand. In that, it later turned out, Score failed. When all the unopened Score wax boxes and all the Score factory set disappeared from the marketplace, demand sent the set from $35 to nearly $70 in the space of about two months, with rookie cards such as Barry Sanders ($15 to $30) and Don Majkowski ($3 to $6.50) also jumping up tremendously.

Why did Score have such a low print run? The cost of printing cards is not as cheap as you'd think. Unlike Topps and Pro Set, Score

1990 Score Neal Anderson — an improved product, but overproduction hurt card values. (Don Butler)

Score's 1989 Don Majkowski — low production and high demand mean expensive rookie cards. (Don Butler)

does not own its own printing press and must contract out to an outside printer, which is also a considerable cost. If Score could keep its costs down while meeting demand, it would do so. A company could lose a lot of money by printing cards nobody would buy. And since Score conceivably doesn't have the financial backing of a company such as Topps, it has to be very careful with the bottom line.

Scarcity and demand are also prime factors in determining prices for cards produced before, say, 1987, but the biggest impact on the price of an older card is condition. Quite simply, the card hobby was not viewed as a money-making business until just a couple of years ago. As explained earlier, cards just weren't taken care of the way they are today. Since older cards are found in a variety of (usually bad) conditions, dealers and hobby publications set up a condition guide or card grading guide, which can break the price of a card down into categories.

Here's a brief rundown of each definition, which has been refined and debated over and refined further since the early 1980s. The entire concept of price guides can be credited to Jim Beckett, who began asking collectors for their input on card pricing in *Sports Collectors Digest* in the early 1980s.

MINT (M)

A perfect card. Well-centered, with equal borders. Four sharp, square corners. No creases, edge dents, surface scratches, paper flaws, loss of luster, yellowing or fading, regardless of age. No imperfectly printed card—out of register or ink flawed—or card stained by contact with gum wax or other substances can be considered Mint, even if new out of the pack.

NEAR MINT (NM)

A nearly perfect card. At first glance, a Near Mint card appears perfect. Upon closer examination, however, a minor flaw will be discovered. On well-centered cards, three of the four corners must be perfectly sharp. A slightly off-center card would also fit this grade, if otherwise perfect.

EXCELLENT (EX)

Corners are still fairly sharp with only moderate wear. Borders may be off-center. No creases. Minor gum, wax, or product stains, front or back. Surfaces may show some loss of luster.

VERY GOOD (VG)

Shows obvious handling. Corners rounded and/or perhaps showing minor creases. Other minor creases may be visible. Surfaces may exhibit loss of luster, but all printing is intact. May show considerable gum, wax or other packaging stains. No major creases, tape marks, or extraneous markings or writing. Card exhibits honest wear, but no damage.

GOOD (G)

A well-worn card with no intentional damage or abuse. May have major or multiple creases. Corners rounded well into borders.

FAIR (F)

Shows excessive wear, along with damage or abuse such as thumb tack holes, evidence of having been taped or pasted, perhaps small tears around edges or creases heavy enough to break the cardboard. Back may have minor added writing or be missing small bits of paper. Still a basically complete card.

POOR (P)

A card that has been tortured to death. Corners or other areas may be missing. Card may have been trimmed, show holes from paper punch or have been used for BB gun practice. Front may have extraneous pen or pencil writing or other defacement. Major portions on front or back design may be missing. Not a pretty sight.

In addition to these seven widely used grading terms, collectors will often encounter intermediate grades such as VG-EX (Very Good to Excellent), EX-MT (Excellent to Mint), or NR MT-MT (Near Mint to Mint). These terms are used to describe a card with all the characteristics of a lower grade, with enough of those of the higher grade to merit mention. The pricing of a card with one of these labels falls midway between each grade.

So how does a price grade analyst arrive at a card price? That part is easy. He reports the price the market is willing to pay for a card. But how does he find that price? That's a little tougher. That means reading trade publications—especially ads, because dealers have a clearer pulse on the supply and demand—and they go to shows. He watches teletype, if available. He talks to dealers who tell him what's moving and how fast. By then, he should have a pretty clear picture of card prices.

Of course, that's hardly a perfect method. A card price can skyrocket in a week, while it's at least two weeks between pricing and actual publication of the price list.

Still, with all of this information in mind—condition of a card, scarcity, and demand—a price guide coordinator can give a fairly accurate list of what your cards are worth. Price guide analysts have a pretty good idea of what's scarce and can make some basic assumptions as to the condition of the majority of cards (for instance, that most football cards before 1972 can usually be found in Near Mint condition at best), the main job for a price guide analyst is determining prices by surveys.

In the case of the *Sports Collectors Digest* football card price guide, dealers and collectors around the country are periodically contacted to determine the values of those cards. It's not as massive an undertaking as it may seem, since the recent year's cards are the only ones that jump up and down in price seemingly from week to week. Older cards usually hold their value and slowly creep up or down in value.

Because there are so many football card price guides out there—since the football boom of 1989, at least six price guides have been published—prices are bound to be different because the method of determining prices is different. In some smaller price guides and in those published in a certain region of the country, prices may be more localized—in other words, stars who played college or pro ball in the area will receive a higher list price. The price isn't wrong; it's just a regional price. For instance, you can expect to pay a higher price for a Walter Payton rookie card in Chicago than you would for the same card in San Francisco. A regionalized price guide reflects this.

We briefly touched on the categories of collectors/investors, so it may be a good idea to profile each here. We've broken them down into three divisions: the strict collector, the collector/dealer, and the investor.

The collector, to quote the obvious hoary cliche, is the backbone of the hobby. Without the collector there would be no cards. Sportscards collectors have been around for well over a hundred years.

The collector is interested in obtaining cards in basically any condition. If he/she needs a Johnny Unitas third-year card to complete a collection, chances are the card doesn't have to be in Near Mint shape. Creases don't daunt the collector—the prize is getting the card, scouring over the bio notes and stats, and completing the set. Trading is a primary interest to collectors, because that's how you meet other collectors. Dollar value doesn't figure into trades—you can swap forty Pro Set doubles for the fifteen Fleer you need to complete a set. Selling a card is almost unthinkable for the collector. It means long nights of pining over the decision and actually having to sweat about the monetary worth of a card.

The collector/dealer has no such qualms about selling. He/she has dozens of doubles of a particular card, and worries only if the price will skyrocket on them once they're sold. The prime difference between a strict collector and a collector/dealer is grading—the collector/dealer is out for cards in better condition. The collector/dealer buys a lot of cards and still trades, but sells a lot of cards to support his hobby.

The investor's prime concern is condition and demand. Most investors today, as explained elsewhere, look either for several hundred-count lots of rookie cards or high-grade (NM-plus) pre-1980 cards. All are strictly for investment only, bought in the trust the card will escalate in value like a stock and will be sold for much more than it was originally bought.

While there's nothing inherently wrong in any of the three categories, the investment angle makes it tough for the collector to find any good deals on old material. The trend in the past two years has the collector all but shut out of the pre-1970s market (except for longing looks at dealer tables) and has restricted collector buying to only new issues.

Investing and speculating has as you well know, created astounding divisions in card pricing. Cards in strict Mint condition—a perfect card—are rarely listed before 1970, simply because few of them are out there. Those that actually changed hands have commended prices that far exceed any book price. Cards in Near Mint condition are often much closer to the prices listed in the guides.

Pricing has become far more scientific than it was even six years ago. Now that collectors are much more aware of price, it's easier to determine and list prices for your cards.

Taking Care of Your Cards

Football cards do more than just help us preserve the past. They are more than just an investment. Looking at a Terry Bradshaw card may evoke memories and personal recollections of the glory days when the black and gold of the Pittsburgh Steelers awoke a nation to its native sons, the laborers.

There is history on the backs of the cards as we read through to find out more about the league in its early years. There are teams of yesteryear that no longer play on Sundays. There are players who through the years have become sports heroes and legends of the game we love.

With this in mind, it is quite important that your cards don't become memories of the past. This means that your cards should be taken care of and protected from potential damage.

Many times you'll see friends with collections of great value, yet because of years of wear their card bring only a fraction of their current value. Here are some tips for protecting your cards.

Pacific's 1991 Joe Montana. Montana is a sure HOFer, so always keep his card in good condition.

PROTECTIVE HOLDERS

If you have a card that is very special to you because of its player or value, it should be housed in a protective holder. There are a variety of protective holders on the market today. Most hobby shops have them available. If you are in an area with a card store, check one of the hobby publications.

Protective holders keep the general wear and tear your card suffers to a bare minimum. You can view the cards from both sides and they, the holders, are generally thought of as one of the keys to the current supplies available to the hobby.

Not every card needs to be housed inside a protective holder. The holders cost is in the twenty-cent to fifty-cent range; thus only cards with value need to be kept in these. These vinyl sleeves are lightweight and great for storage. There are semi-rigid sleeve holders and rigid holders. The semi-rigid are the least expensive and they tend to bend slightly. That's okay, but if you have a doubt you can always seek the advice of your hobby shop owner.

Also in this same line of holders are the heavy plastic holders that have come in two varieties, both screw down and snap tight. These are the most expensive way of securing a card.

There are reasons, however, for wanting to purchase one of the more expensive plastic holders. If you are displaying a card or handle it frequently and if the card has great value, then this is your best bet. For example, if you have a Gale Sayers rookie card in Mint condition and you would like your friends to be able to see it when they come to visit, then use one of the more expensive card holders.

ALBUMS

Like most every product made today, there are good and bad albums on the market. Remembering that there has always been a certain value growth in football cards, it is good to purchase a quality album to keep your cards.

You can also get different sized albums. The top of the line is the three-inch spine with the D-shaped ring.

There are two-inch spines that are also okay, but to get a full set of the large number of cards being produced in today's sets, you most likely need the three-inch size.

There are albums with designs and they come in all types of colors, just in case you prefer one color to another.

SHEETS

If you found the album that you want to store your cards in, the next thing you'll need are sheets to store your cards. This used to be a relatively easy thing, but recently problems have arisen from the use of certain chemicals to make the sheets. The chemical PVC has caused some cards to change color and now it is thought of as a risk.

The stock that football cards are printed on is porous and the oil that is given off by the polyvinyl chloride (PVC) can make your once valuable cards worthless.

Today, most all companies are using chemicals other than PVC to make their sheets. But when purchasing sheets, be careful to check them out and if unsure, ask.

Sheets today vary in cost because of the brand and the type of sheet. Vinyl is still the king of the hill, but there are also polyethyl-

Pacific's 1991 Eric Metcalf. Kept properly, this promising running back's card may be worth a great deal someday. (Chuck Bennett)

ene sheets and poly-pro sheets. Most card shops charge about twenty cents per page, but they can be purchased cheaper in larger quantities.

The most popular card sheet today is the nine pocket sheet for regular sized cards. Each sheet can hold either nine or eighteen cards, if you chose to put them back-to-back. Putting your cards back-to-back will not harm them, but you can not view the backs of the cards.

For different size cards, there are different sheets. The older Bowman football cards need the eight pocket sheets. There are also twelve pocket sheets, six pocket sheets, four pocket sheets, two pockets sheets and even one pocket sheets.

Sheets differ by the way you load the cards into them. There are top loading pages and side loading pages. Some sheets also come with pre-punched holes; making them easier to put into your albums.

When it comes to the number of pages per album, there is no clear-cut rule. Put in as many as you need without overdoing it.

The more pages you put into an album, the more weight it has to carry and the easier it is for them to break.

BOXES

If you are a set collector and you buy complete factory sets, then your only concern is to keep your sets in a safe and dry place. If you, however, collate sets yourself, you'll need to use boxes to store your sets. Most of the set boxes are made from quality cardboard and are perfect for storing your cards.

Another tip is to keep your commons or loose cards in monster boxes. Monster boxes come in a variety of sizes from 2,500 to 8,000 count. The two-piece boxes seem to be the best. Keeping your cards in these boxes keeps them out of the way of Mom and your little sister who might find bending cards a new hobby.

Whatever you chose to do, do something. It has taken you a fair amount of work and plenty of money to put together a nice football collection. Be responsible and take care of your cards. Even taking care of your commons in monster boxes is a good

Pacific's 1991 Troy Aikman. In 1989, Aikman was the NFL's first pick. Keep an eye on card values and keep Aikman in Mint condition. (Chuck Bennett)

idea. Jeff Hostetler may be a common card today, but what about tomorrow?

INSURANCE

Okay, you might think you are a bit young to be worrying about insurance. Or you might think that your collection is too small or not valuable enough for insurance. Here are a number of tips when considering insurance. Whether you take insurance or not, it should at least be considered.

One thing to always remember is to keep good records. Keep up with what you paid for your cards in some type of notebook or binder. The date when you bought it, its appraised value and its current value are all important pieces of information that insurance people will want to know in case of fire or theft.

The next step is to talk to your current agent about his company's policy in regards to card collections. If you have a standard homeowners policy, there is a good chance that your collection is not covered. Unless you specifically tell your agent that you needed coverage on these items, they may have gone unnoticed. You may want to check about a floater or even a separate insurance policy on your cards depending on the size and value of your collection.

For example, the standard homeowners policy covers both the home and it contents. If the home is valued at $70,000, then you can expect your contents to be insured for about $35,000. That means that all of your personal articles are included in the $35,000. Your furniture, clothes, antiques, and other possession might add up to that figure alone and yet you'll receive no additional monies even if your collection was valued at $10,000.

The floater that can be added to your insurance is designed for specific items such as your collection. You will have to itemize much of your collection and be able to show records for proof of value. Carefully look at this policy to see if it replaces the cards in cases of theft, fire, flood, tornado, etc.

If you have a collection that exceeds the value of $35,000 or more then you'll want to get a valuable article policy. This is much like the fine art policies that cover paintings, fine antiques, and jewelry. Expect to pay between $500 and $700 for a yearly premium. Though the cost seems high, the risk that you take for a collection this valuable is much higher.

Some other things to keep in mind are to always update your collection. Insurance companies need to know when you add a 1935 National Chicle set to your collection. If in doubt ask your agent. If he is unaware he can call his state or national office to get the information that you need. Be smart, be insured!

Conclusion: The Future of Football Cards

In the last two years, the explosion in football cards has added a whole new dimension to the collecting hobby. Thanks to innovative techniques in marketing by Pro Set, a breakthrough in tapping the collector vein by Score's inclusion of first-round draft picks in 1989, the return to football by Fleer, the expanded Topps sets, and a new dimension in card quality by Action Packed, football card collectors have just as much to look forward to as baseball card collectors. This is evidenced by the large number of price guides which list football, basketball and hockey prices in addition to—and sometimes exclusively of—baseball card prices.

It currently appears as if the trend in collecting is heading back toward "seasonal" collecting. In the mid 1960s and 1970s, a kid would buy baseball cards in the spring, football cards in the fall, and basketball and hockey cards in the winter. There's been a return to that style of collecting for many card buyers, but now it's football in the spring, hockey in the summer, and basketball and baseball in the fall. There have never been as many collectors in the hobby as there are today. Nor has there

1989 Score was the first company to include first-round draft picks from the same year.

ever been such an incredible number of cards, card companies, and quality memorabilia.

Right now, the future looks excellent for the survival of the football memorabilia hobby. Of course you expect us to say that, but there's good evidence to support that claim. Sports in America has become its own culture. Even in times of recession, Americans will continue to follow and watch sports as sort of a national diversion, a communal meeting where your fantasies and good versus evil tendencies are always indulged. Because we have such an affinity for sports, we will continue to buy the product in its myriad forms— videos, clothing, and cards.

The number of kids entering the hobby also can't be ignored. Since many of them are keenly aware of card shows and card values, chances are excellent they will stick with the hobby as long as it remains fun and profitable. Card collecting is cool, no matter what your age.

You look at the breadth and depth of the hobby—equipment, card variations, programs, Canadian Football League, books,

1990 Jogo CFL football
card: another quality
collectible.

Programs are underrated
football collectibles. (Don
Butler)

autographs—and the future does look good. The entire hobby is keyed on the popularity of pro football, which is solidly entrenched as an autumn Sunday exercise for most Americans. There's something about waking up early to toss the football around with your friends or your kids, then heading back in the house to watch a variety of pre-game shows before your team hits the tube. Every game counts. Rivalries seem to get more intense each year. Lower round draft picks leap into superstardom, catching all observers by surprise. Each season has a different trick or accidental play that makes the highlight film. The usually silent July training camps and uncertainty end with hundreds of millions of spectators on Super Bowl Sunday in late January.

We think we've entered a whole new age in card collecting.

Appendix A
A List of Pro Football Hall of Famers and Their First, Second, and Last-Year Cards with Prices

This list of Hall of Famers lists players and coaches only. Contributors, front office people such as Bert Bell, Dan Reeves, Lamar Hunt, and Pete Rozelle are not included. If a Hall of Famer was a player and a coach, his last card listed will be that of a player, since it carries more value. For many of the charter members and old-time players, a regular-card was not issued during his playing days. His first card may have been issued in the Fleer Hall of Fame sets, the Football Immortals sets, and the Swell Hall of Fame sets. If this is the case, he does not have a "true" rookie card; this will be noted under his last card by "etc." Therefore, since he does not have a true rookie or second-year card, he'll never have a "true" last issue card, since none of the cards were issued during his playing days. One other note: in 1952, Bowman released the same cards in both a large size and in a small size. Values for Bowman Large are much greater than it is for their smaller counterparts. Prices listed will be from the Bowman Small set.

(Key: B—Bowman; C—National Chicle; FI—Football Immortal; F1—Fleer; L—Leaf; Ph—Philadelphia; S—Swell; T—Topps; *—deceased)

Player	Year of Induction	Rookie Card/ Price	2nd Card Price	Last/ Price
Herb Adderly	1980	1964 Ph #71 $ 35.00	1965 Ph #72 $ 7.50	1973 T #243 $ 2.50
Lance Alworth	1978	1963 FI #72 90.00	1964 T #155 22.50	1973 T #61 3.00
Doug Atkins	1982	1954 B #4 20.00	1960 T #20 5.00	1969 T #105 3.50
Red Badgro	1981	1985 FI #9 .50	1988 S #9 .20	etc
*Cliff Battles	1968	1935 C #10 125.00	1974 F #1 .90	etc
Sammy Baugh	1963	1948 B #22 325.00 1948 L #34 225.00	1949 L #26 135.00	1952 B #30 185.00
Chuck Bednarik	1967	1948 L #54 175.00	1949 L #134 65.00	1961 T #101 5.00
Bobby Bell	1983	1964 T #90 20.00	1965 T #91 20.00	1975 T #281 1.50
Raymond Berry (1)	1973	1957 T #94 75.00	1958 T #120 14.00	1967 Ph #14 3.50
Fred Biletnikoff	1988	1965 T #133 100.00	1966 T #104 27.50	1979 T #305 1.25
George Blanda	1981	1954 B #23 500.00	1955 B #62 90.00	1976 T #355 4.50
Mel Blount	1989	1975 T #12 10.00	1976 T #480 3.50	1983 T #357 .20
Terry Bradshaw	1989	1971 T #156 100.00	1972 T #150 27.50	1984 T #162 .90
Jim Brown	1971	1958 T #62 700.00	1959 T #10 175.00	1966 Ph #41 50.00

Player	Year of Induction	Rookie Card / Price	2nd Card Price	Last / Price
Paul Brown	1967	1952 B #14 $ 70.00	1974 Fl #5 $ 1.00	etc
Roosevelt Brown	1975	1956 T #41 25.00	1957 T #11 10.00	1966 Ph #119 $ 3.75
Willie Brown	1984	1965 T #46 40.00	1970 T #144 4.50	1975 T #95 1.50
Buck Buchanan	1990	1964 T #92 20.00	1965 T #94 20.00	1975 T #16 1.50
Dick Butkus	1979	1966 Ph #31 95.00	1967 Ph #28 27.50	1974 T #230 4.75
Earl Campbell	1991	1979 T #390 30.00	1979 T #390 30.00	etc
Tony Canadeo	1974	1950 B #9 35.00	1951 B #90 20.00	1951 B #90 20.00
*Guy Chamberlin	1965	1974 Fl #7 .75	1975 Fl #5 .50	etc
*Jack Christiansen	1970	1952 B #129 55.00	1954 B #100 12.50	1958 T #70 6.50
*Dutch Clark	1963	1935 NC #1 500.00	1935 NC #1 500.00	etc
George Connor	1975	1948 L #347 35.00	1949 L #40 25.00	1954 B #116 12.50
*Jimmy Conzelman	1964	1974 Fl #9 .75	1975 Fl #8 .35	etc
Larry Csonka	1987	1969 T #120 65.00	1970 T #162 20.00	1980 T #485 1.25
Willie Davis	1981	1964 Ph #72 35.00	1965 Ph #73 7.50	1967 Ph #76 3.00
Len Dawson	1987	1963 Fl #47 90.00	1964 T #96 60.00	1976 T #308 2.50
Mike Ditka	1988	1962 T #17 95.00	1963 T #62 22.50	1968 T #162 5.50

Player	Year of Induction	Rookie Card/ Price	2nd Card Price	Last/ Price
Art Donovan	1968	1952 B #46 $ 70.00	1956 T #36 $ 12.50	1961 Fl #39 $ 4.50
*John "Paddy" Driscoll	1965	1974 Fl #11 .75	1975 Fl #75 .35	etc
Bill Dudley	1966	1948 L #36 40.00 1948 B #80 75.00	1949 L #22 25.00	1951 B #144 45.00
*Turk Edwards	1969	1935 NC #11 125.00	1955 T #36 27.50	1955 T #36 27.50
Weeb Ewbank	1978	1985 Fl #39 .35	1988 S #89 .20	etc
Tom Fears	1970	1950 B #51 60.00	1951 B #6 22.50	1956 T #42 12.50
Ray Flaherty	1976	1985 Fl #21 .35	1988 S #21 .20	etc
*Len Ford	1976	1955 B #14 25.00	1957 T #147 10.00	1957 T #147 10.00
Dan Fortmann	1965	1974 Fl #13 .75	1975 Fl #20 .50	etc
Frank Gatski	1985	1955 B #119 20.00	1955 B #119 20.00	1955 B #119 20.00
*Bill George	1974	1956 T #47 22.50	1958 T #119 6.50	1963 T #70 4.00
Frank Gifford	1977	1952 B #16 650.00	1953 B #43 275.00	1964 Ph #117 42.50
Sid Gillman	1983	1960 Fl #7 6.00	1960 Fl #7 6.00	1960 Fl #7 6.00
Otto Graham	1965	1950 B #45 500.00	1951 B #2 100.00	1954 B #40 55.00
Red Grange	1963	1955 T #27 250.00	1974 Fl #15 1.75	etc

Player	Year of Induction	Rookie Card/ Price	2nd Card Price	Last/ Price
Joe Greene	1987	1971 T #245 $ 30.00	1972 T #230 $ 7.50	1981 T #495 $ .75
Forrest Gregg	1977	1959 T #56 12.50	1961 Fl #94 4.00	1967 Ph #77 2.50
Bob Griese	1990	1968 T #196 55.00	1969 T #161 15.00	1981 T #482 1.25
Lou Groza	1974	1950 B #6 125.00	1951 B #75 50.00	1963 T #19 12.50
*Joe Guyon	1966	1975 Fl #51 .75	1985 Fl #47 .50	etc
*George Halas	1963	1952 B #48 75.00	1964 Ph #28 5.00	1965 Ph #28 7.50
Jack Ham	1988	1973 T #115 9.00	1974 T #137 3.00	1982 T #210 .45
John Hannah	1991	1974 T #383 4.50	1975 T #318 2.00	1986 T #36 .20
Franco Harris	1990	1973 T #89 37.50	1974 T #220 9.00	1984 T #165 .50
*Ed Healey	1964	1975 Fl #55 .50	1985 Fl #49 .35	etc
Mel Hein	1963	1955 T #28 22.50	1974 Fl #17 .75	etc
Ted Hendricks	1990	1972 T #93 12.50	1973 T #430 4.00	1984 T #110 .30
Wilbur "Pete" Henry	1963	1955 T #100 250.00	1974 Fl #18 .75	etc
*Arnie Herber	1966	1975 Fl #75 .75	1985 Fl #52 .50	etc
*Bill Hewitt	1971	1974 Fl #75 .75	1985 Fl #16 .50	etc

Player	Year of Induction	Rookie Card/ Price	2nd Card Price	Last/ Price
*Clarke Hinkle	1964	1935 NC #24 $ 125.00	1974 Fl #20 $ 1.00	etc
Elroy Hirsch	1968	1950 B #52 75.00	1951 B #76 22.50	1957 T #46 $ 10.00
Paul Hornung	1986	1957 T #151 650.00	1959 T #82 37.50	1967 Ph #123 12.50
Ken Houston	1986	1971 T #113 13.00	1972 T #78 4.50	1980 T #145 .50
*Cal Hubbard	1963	1974 Fl #22 1.25	1975 Fl #17 .65	etc
Sam Huff	1982	1959 T #51 47.50	1960 T #80 5.00	1965 Ph #187 5.00
Don Hutson	1963	1955 T #97 125.00	1974 Fl #24 1.50	etc
John Henry Johnson	1987	1955 B #42 22.50	1957 T #16 10.00	1965 Ph #147 4.50
David "Deacon" Jones	1980	1963 T #44 35.00	1965 Ph #89 6.50	1974 T #390 2.00
Stan Jones	1991	1956 T #71 10.00	1957 T #71 5.00	1962 T #18 4.50
Sonny Jurgensen	1983	1958 T #90 125.00	1961 T #95 12.50	1975 T #2 1.00
*Walt Kiesling	1966	1975 Fl #74 .75	1985 Fl #62 .50	etc
Jack Lambert	1990	1976 T #220 12.50	1977 T #480 3.50	1985 T #357 .50
Earl "Curley" Lambeau	1963	1974 Fl #25 1.25	1975 Fl #31 .75	etc
Dick "Night Train" Lane	1974	1957 T #85 30.00	1961 Fl #84 4.50	1964 Ph #61 4.00

Player	Year of Induction	Rookie Card/ Price	2nd Card Price	Last/ Price
Tom Landry	1990	1951 B #20 $ 575.00	1952 B #142 $ 250.00	1989 Sc #330 $ 3.00
Jim Langer	1987	1973 T #341 7.50	1974 T #397 2.50	1979 T #425 .40
Willie Lanier	1986	1971 T #114 13.00	1972 T #35 4.50	1977 T #155 1.00
Yale Lary	1979	1952 B #140 50.00	1957 T #68 7.50	1965 Ph #63 4.00
Dante Lavelli	1975	1950 B #78 40.00	1951 B #73 20.00	1954 B #111 10.00
Bobby Layne	1967	1948 L #6 190.00	1949 L #67 75.00	1962 T #127 13.50
Alphonse "Tuffy" Leemans	1978	1985 Fl #69 .35	1988 S #69 .20	etc
Bob Lilly	1980	1963 T #82 75.00	1964 Ph #48 17.50	1975 T #175 3.00
*Vince Lombardi	1971	1964 Ph #84 30.00	1965 Ph #84 7.50	1965 Ph #84 7.50
Sid Luckman	1965	1948 L #1 225.00 1948 B #107 150.00	1949 L #15 100.00	1950 B #27 45.00
William Roy "Link" Lyman	1964	1975 Fl #52 1.00	1985 Fl #73 .35	etc
Gino Marchetti	1972	1952 B #23 65.00	1957 T #5 12.50	1964 Ph #4 4.00
Ollie Matson	1972	1952 B #127 70.00	1954 B #12 15.00	1962 T #79 13.50
Don Maynard	1987	1961 T #150 37.50 1961 Fl #215 55.00	1962 Fl #59 15.00	1973 T #175 2.50

Player	Year of Induction	Rookie Card/ Price	2nd Card Price	Last/ Price
George McAfee	1966	1948 L #19 $ 50.00 1940 B #95 75.00	1949 L #41 $ 25.00	1949 L #41 $ 25.00
Mike McCormack	1984	1955 B #2 25.00	1956 T #105 7.50	1963 T #17 7.00
Hugh McElhenny	1970	1952 B #29 65.00	1953 B #32 22.50	1963 T #103 5.00
Johnny "Blood" McNally	1963	1974 Fl #33 1.25	1975 Fl #13 .80	etc
August "Mike" Michalske	1964	1975 Fl #56 .50	1985 Fl #82 .35	etc
Wayne Millner	1968	1952 B #57 35.00	1952 B #57 35.00	1952 B #57 35.00
Bobby Mitchell	1983	1959 T #140 17.50	1960 T #25 5.00	1969 T #114 3.50
Ron Mix	1979	1960 Fl #118 20.00	1961 Fl #162 10.00 1961 T #168 6.00	1969 T #99
Lenny Moore	1975	1956 T #60 65.00	1957 T #128 20.00	1966 Ph #21 4.50
Marion Motley	1968	1950 B #43 60.00	1951 B #109 22.50	1953 B #9 20.00
George Musso	1982	1985 Fl #88 .35	1988 S #88 .15	etc
*Bronko Nagurski	1963	1935 NC #34 4,600.00	1974 Fl #35 3.50	etc
Joe Namath	1985	1965 T #122 1,350.00	1966 T #96 250.00	1973 T #400 20.00

Player	Year of Induction	Rookie Card/ Price	2nd Card Price	Last/ Price
Earle "Greasy" Neale	1969	1975 Fl #69 $ .50	1985 Fl #90 $ .35	etc
*Ernie Nevers	1963	1955 T #56 22.50	1974 Fl #36 1.25	etc
Ray Nitschke	1978	1963 T #96 50.00	1965 Ph #79 10.00	1971 T #133 $ 4.00
Leo Nomellini	1969	1948 L #52 125.00	1950 B #107 30.00	1963 T #143 4.50
Merlin Olsen	1982	1964 Ph #91 75.00	1965 Ph #94 20.00	1975 T #525 2.00
Jim Otto	1980	1961 Fl #197 25.00 1961 T #182 22.50	1962 Fl #72 12.50	1975 T #497 1.50
Steve Owen	1966	1952 B #4 27.50	1952 B #4 27.50	1952 B #4 27.50
Alan Page	1988	1970 T #59 12.50	1971 T #71 4.00	1982 T #292 .75
Clarence "Ace" Parker	1972	1955 T #84 35.00	1975 Fl #38 .75	etc
Joe Perry	1969	1950 B #35 75.00	1951 B #105 22.50	1962 T #4 5.00
Pete Pihos	1970	1948 L #16 45.00 1948 B #63 150.00	1949 L #28 25.00	1955 B #10 9.00
Jim Ringo	1981	1955 B #70 27.50	1958 T #103 6.50	1966 Ph #141 4.00
Andy Robustelli	1971	1952 B #85 50.00	1955 B #121 12.50	1962 T #108 5.00

Player	Year of Induction	Rookie Card/ Price	2nd Card Price	Last/ Price
Gayle Sayers	1977	1966 Ph #38 $ 200.00	1967 Ph #35 $ 65.00	1972 T #110 $ 25.00
Joe Schmidt	1973	1956 T #44 40.00	1958 Ph #3 8.50	1964 Ph #66 3.50
Tex Schramm	1991	1991 PS #30 .15	etc	etc
Art Shell	1989	1973 T #77 12.50	1974 T #272 2.50	1982 T #198 .50
O.J. Simpson	1985	1970 T #90 175.00	1971 T #260 40.00	1979 T #170 4.50
Bob St. Clair	1990	1955 B #101 22.50	1957 T #18 7.50	1964 Ph #164 2.50
Bart Starr	1977	1957 T #119 700.00	1958 T #66 150.00	1971 T #200 17.50
Roger Staubach	1985	1972 T #200 80.00	1973 T #475 22.50	1980 T #331 1.00
Ernie Stautner	1969	1951 B #96 50.00	1954 B #118 17.50	1963 T #129 7.50
Jan Stenerud	1991	1970 T #25 6.00	1971 T #61 2.50	1985 T #98 .20
*Ken Strong	1967	1935 NC #7 150.00	1955 T #24 12.50	1955 T #24 12.50
Joe Stydahar	1967	1952 B #99 35.00	1952 B #99 35.00	1952 B #99 35.00
Fran Tarkenton	1986	1962 T #90 475.00	1963 T #98 85.00	1979 T #200 3.50
Charley Taylor	1984	1965 Ph #195 37.50	1966 Ph #194 6.00	1976 T #450 1.00
Jim Taylor (2)	1976	1959 T #155 12.50	1960 T #52 5.00	1968 T #160 5.50
*Jim Thorpe	1963	1955 T #37 400.00	1955 T #37 400.00	1955 T #37 400.00

Player	Year of Induction	Rookie Card/ Price	2nd Card Price	Last/ Price
Y.A. Tittle	1974	1950 B #5 $ 225.00	1951 B #32 $ 70.00	1964 Ph #124 $ 15.00
*George Trafton	1964	1975 Fl #53 .75	1985 Fl #116 .35	etc
Charley Trippi	1968	1948 B #17 85.00 1948 L #29 45.00	1949 L #16 27.50	1955 B #139 12.50
*Emlen Tunnell	1967	1951 B #91 50.00	1952 B #39 30.00	1958 T #42 6.50
Bulldog Turner	1966	1948 L #3 65.00 1948 B #36 175.00	1949 L #150 65.00	1951 B #13 20.00
Johnny Unitas	1979	1957 T #138 900.00	1958 T #22 275.00	1974 T #150 9.50
Gene Upshaw	1987	1972 T #186 12.50	1973 T #50 3.50	1981 T #219 .50
*Norm Van Brocklin	1971	1951 B #4 125.00	1952 B #1 325.00	1957 T #22 20.00
Steve Van Buren	1965	1948 B #7 125.00 1948 L #22 85.00	1949 L #79 40.00	1952 B #45 25.00
Doak Walker	1986	1948 L #4 65.00	1950 B #1 70.00	1955 B #1 45.00
Paul Warfield	1983	1965 Ph #41 45.00	1967 Ph #46 6.50	1977 T #185 1.00
*Bob Waterfield	1965	1948 B #26 150.00 1948 L #26 85.00	1949 L #89 40.00	1952 B #137 30.00
Arnie Weinmeister	1984	1951 B #21 25.00	1952 B #101 25.00	1952 B #101 25.00

Player	Year of Induction	Rookie Card / Price	2nd Card Price	Last / Price
Bill Willis	1977	1985 FI #126 $ .35	1988 S #126 $ .20	etc
Larry Wilson	1978	1963 T #155 20.00	1966 Ph #168 5.00	1972 T #205 $ 3.00
Alex Wojciechowicz	1968	1948 B #61 85.00	1955 T #82 17.50	1955 T #82 17.50
Willie Wood	1989	1963 T #95 25.00	1964 Ph #82 5.00	1971 T #55 3.50

1. Photos on last-year card actually shows Bob Boyd.
2. Photos on first and second year cards actually show Cardinal linebacker Jim Taylor.

Appendix B
Addresses and Contacts

NFL teams usually send free schedules, occasional stickers, and some catalogues through the mail. When writing directly to a team for this information, include a self addressed, stamped envelope, which makes a response much more likely. Addresses for each team are listed below. If you're writing to a team for information, address your request to the publicity department. If you're attempting to get an autograph of the player, address to him in care of the team.

Atlanta Falcons I-85 and Suwanee Road, Suwanee, GA 30174.

Buffalo Bills One Bills Drive, Orchard Park, NY 14127.

Chicago Bears 250 N. Washington Rd., Lake Forest, IL 60045.

Cincinnati Bengals 200 Riverfront Stadium, Cincinnati, OH 45202.

Cleveland Browns Tower B. Cleveland Stadium, Cleveland, OH 44114.

Dallas Cowboys One Cowboys Parkway, Irving, TX 75063.

Denver Broncos 13655 East Dove Valley Parkway, Englewood, CO 80112.

Detroit Lions Pontiac Silverdome, 1200 Featherstone Rd., Pontiac, MI 48057.

Green Bay Packers 1265 Lombardi Ave., Green Bay, WI 54307.

Houston Oilers 6910 Fannin St., Houston, TX 77030.

Indianapolis Colts 7001 W 56th St., Indianapolis, IN 46254.

Kansas City Chiefs Arrowhead Stadium, Kansas City, MO 64129.

Los Angeles Raiders 332 Center St., El Segundo, CA 90245.

Los Angeles Rams 2327 W, Lincoln Ave., Anaheim, CA 92801.

Miami Dolphins Joe Robbie Stadium, 2269 NW 199th St., Miami, FL 33056.

Minnesota Vikings 9520 Viking Dr., Eden Prairie, MN 55344.

New England Patriots Sullivan Stadium, Route 1, Foxboro, MA 02035.

New Orleans Saints 1500 Paydras St., New Orleans, LA 70112.

New York Giants Giants Stadium, East Rutherford, NJ 07073.

New York Jets 1000 Fulton Ave., Hempstead, NY 11550.

Philadelphia Eagles Veterans Stadium, Broad Street and Pattison Ave., Philadelphia, PA 19148.

Phoenix Cardinals P.O. Box 888, Phoenix, AZ 85001-0888.

Pittsburgh Steelers 300 Stadium Circle, Pittsburgh, PA 15212.

San Diego Chargers Jack Murphy Stadium, P.O. Box 20666, San Diego, CA 92120.

San Francisco 49ers 4949 Centennial Blvd., Santa Clara, CA 95054.

Seattle Seahawks 11220 NE 53rd St., Kirkland, WA 98033.

Tampa Bay Buccaneers One Buccaneer Place, Tampa, FL 33607.

Washington Redskins Dulles International Airport, P.O. Box 17247, Washington, D.C. 20041.

The Pro Football Hall of Fame's gift shop offers a number of collectibles and may be able to send you a catalog. If you're looking for an autograph of a Hall of Famer and the Hall is able to forward mail to the player, you can write the Hall care of the player and a "please forward" message on the envelope (don't forget the SASE to improve your chances for a response). You can write to the Hall at 2121 George Halas Drive NW, Canton, OH 44708.

If you bought damaged cards (current release only—don't try it with any of last year's cards) and you'd like them replaced, most of the card companies are able to accommodate you. You can write to them and tell them what you think of their products at the addresses listed below. Pro Set also gives out a free Pro Set Gazette twice a year; ask to be put on the mailing list for that.

Action Packed, c/o LBC Sports, 851 North Villa Ave., Suite 101, Villa Park, IL 60181

Bowman Company—see Topps

Fleer Corporation 10th Somerville, Philadelphia, PA 19141

Goal Line Art P.O. Box 372, Ridley Park, PA 19078

Jogo Incorporated 1872 Queensdale Ave., Gloucester, Ontario, Canada K1T 1K1

Pacific Trading Cards 18424 Highway 99 Lynnwood, WA 98037

Pro Set Incorporated 15303 Dallas Parkway, Dallas, TX 75248.

Score 25 Ford Road, Westport, CT 06880

Swell Philadelphia Chewing Gum Corp., Havertown, PA 19083-2198

Topps Gum Company 254 36th St., Brooklyn, NY 11232

Upper Deck 23705 Via Del Rio, Yorba Linda, CA 92686

Several publications list football card values and carry stories about football cards. We're trying to be completely objective, but we believe *Sports Collectors Digest*, a weekly magazine, is the best. Don Butler prices the football cards for that magazine, writes a football card report dealing with all the errors, variations, pricing, and questions that are filtered through the *SCD* offices, and edits several accompanying articles on football cards. Chuck Bennett's monthly "Gridiron Gossip" column also runs in *SCD*. The football guide is published once or twice a month in *SCD*. Krause Publications, which publishes *SCD*, also issues a monthly magazine containing football prices and articles, called the Football/Basketball/Hockey Collector.

The other top quality football publications are published by Beckett Publications. They issue a football card price guide twelve times a year, as well as an annual football card price guide book.

Beckett Publications 4887 Alpha Road, Suite 200, Dallas, TX 75244

Football/Basketball/Hockey Collector 700 E. State St., Iola, WI 54990

Sports Collectors Digest 700 E. State St., Iola, WI 54990